HIRE
POWER

Daily Tips & Insights to Boost
Your Hiring Success

HIRE
POWER

Daily Tips & Insights to Boost
Your Hiring Success

BETH SMITH

Hire Power: Daily Tips & Insights to Boost Your Hiring Success

ISBN: 978-1-947939-94-3

Book design by AuthorSourceMedia.
Printed by AuthorSourceMedia LLC in the United States of America.
https://www.AuthorSourceMedia.com
https://a-listinterviews.com/

For Katy: The best part of my life is with you. Thank you for your editing, your drive for perfection, and your patience when I jack up the parenting thing. I am the most proud of being your Mama.

And to my Dad, Dave Deison: for all the business coaching, advice and cash flow lessons. I especially thank you for sharing with me not only your successes but also your mistakes. Your support means the world.

INTRODUCTION

How to Hire Better – Tips and Insights!

In the current world's climate of chaos, it is even more important that you hire the right person. No one knows what the post-COVID-19 world is going to look like, and your business will have to be proactive. This starts by making sure your hiring process is as solid and strong as possible ... and that is the goal of this book!

I've written *Hire Power: Daily Tips & Insights to Boost Your Hiring Success* to give you advantages that you may not have considered. Your business doesn't need to face the challenge of underperforming, disruptive, or otherwise ineffective employees—and you want to make sure you don't hire these types of people in the first place.

This book will give you daily reminders of what to do and not to do in your hiring process. You will be reminded to:

- Be patient. Hiring the right person takes time.

- Hold out for that perfect long-term employee who has passion for the position.

- Listen in the interview to ensure that you have all the information you need to make a good decision.

- Quit reading resumes.

- Respond to each applicant in a timely manner.

- Focus on your ideal candidate.

- Remember that you can have whoever you want.

- Stay positive. You can do this. We can help.

Whether you are a CEO, an HR Director for a multi-national corporation or a sole proprietor needing to hire your first employee, your hiring process can make or break your business. My company's sole focus and objective is to help you ensure your hiring process is the best it can be. A-list Interviews Inc. is ready to help you create the hiring process you need—today! In the meantime, this book will give you food for thought regarding who you hire and why you are hiring that individual.

Wishing you hiring success!

Beth Smith

New Year's Resolutions:
Diet, Exercise, Fire Someone?

At the beginning of each New Year, many of us take the opportunity to regroup and redefine goals for our businesses. This is a time that is often filled with renewed energy to get our lives and work in order.

As a part of your New Year's goals, it might also be time to fire that one employee who is not contributing to your company's vision. The impact of an unengaged employee on your business can be catastrophic: decreased productivity, lowered company morale, and miserable working environments have been common complaints by my clients as they come to the decision to dismiss an employee.

I say start the new year fresh! For example, a past client had an employee who consistently gave my client ultimatums. The threats were often, "If you don't do this, then I'll quit." To start, who wants to work with an individual who is constantly threatening? The team was struggling to work with the individual, the employer was unhappy with the performance of the individual, yet the concept of firing and replacing this person seemed daunting and ill-timed. When my client finally became fed up, they did indeed fire the employee. I won't sugar coat the transition. It was hard, uncomfortable, and came at a terrible time, but my client knew this was the right decision for the company.

I have clients who will begin the new year with new employees who are excited about the company, the job, and the new opportunity. Start your new year with a fresh perspective and make a resolution to find the best employees that are the best fit for your business.

Power Thought

New year. New you.
New employee who makes your job easier.

Traditionally in January, people start thinking about cleaning house, both literally and figuratively. Articles pop up online about how to deep clean your dishwasher (is that a thing?), how often to wash your comforter and, of course, a myriad of content about how to be your better self in the new year. At our house, we clean out closets, attack dust mites with a vengeance, and even get the carpets cleaned. We have replaced pillows, bought new rugs for the hallway, and scrubbed the floor tile until it shines! We want to clean out the old to make room for the new!

I also enjoy helping companies "clean house" at work. In January, I often hear from organizations who want to ramp up during the next few months and know that staffing will be critical. Along with replacing the last year's files with this year's in the filing cabinet, many companies also begin to hire for open and new positions. The downfall is that we often do not move into a new space with new tools. We read the article on deep cleaning the dishwasher, then fail to take the steps to actually clean it. In like manner, companies examine the people on their teams and clearly see improvements that must be made, and yet they fail to make them.

This year, I encourage you to review your interview and hiring process. Revamp job descriptions and determine ideal profiles for your positions. The power of refreshment is invigorating; we are often making space for something new. It just feels so good to clean up! My company's mantra has always been that you can't move forward until you clean up the past, and you can't create something new until you make room for it. Here's to a cleaner, more streamlined year!

Power Thought

Review and revamp anytime you feel stagnant;
you will be amazed and energized!

One of my clients had been expressing frustration over her interview process. After listening to her concerns, I responded that the search was going marvelously. She looked at me like I was nuts! I was so certain of our progress because she was learning and thriving throughout the process. She was raising the bar for the people that she desired to hire. She was also beginning to make great decisions regarding the people that she would hire for her business.

I responded to her look by letting her know that she would not need me for much longer because she was becoming a phenomenal interviewer.

She replied, "Oh! You're like Nanny McPhee who said, "When you need me, but do not want me, I must stay. When you want me, but do not need me, I must go."

My mission for A-list Interviews is to teach people how to successfully choose great people for their teams. It can be a bit frustrating and trying, but once this is accomplished, my clients have their own magic to tap into. I then confidently move on to the next employer or hiring manager in need. Nanny McPhee and I both walk into stressful situations and leave behind a peaceful, productive environment. Are you ready for my help?

Power Thought

Have patience with yourself and your process when you
are on a learning curve.

In every interview process that I have facilitated, there is always a point where my client turns to me and says "I HATE this process." I always warn them before we begin that at some point, they will get frustrated. This usually happens when we have been working together through a series of interviews and my clients raise the bar on the people that they wish to hire, which is the goal behind A-list Interviews.

There is an inevitable delay between the "hiring bar" being raised and the moment when higher caliber people begin to show up, causing the employer to wonder if the A-list candidate will *ever* appear. In other words, they begin to doubt. They doubt the process, themselves, their work, and the candidates.

I love this point in the training and coaching process. We are literally in the darkness that lies before the light, and their A-list person is right around the corner. My clients have all said in one way or another, "I doubt we are going to find this person." I say, "Doubt the doubt." If you are doubtful anyway, then doubt the doubt, not the process. Your ideal candidate is about to walk right through the door. It is miraculous!

Power Thought

Admit your doubts and push through ...
success is closer than you think.

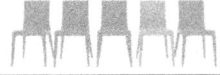

I have a client who asks candidates this interview question: "If you were a type of cheese, which would it be?" The question makes each person laugh and he's had some pretty clever responses such as: "Pepper Jack; I'm spicy!" and "Any of them except blue cheese, because that one stinks!"

For a cheese maker, a chef and perhaps a dairy farmer, this question might be appropriate. Perhaps even a marketing position could warrant this question as the hiring manager might be measuring a person's creativity. However, for most industries and positions, the information gained by asking that question is just like Swiss cheese—full of holes. How does a description of cheese really evaluate the candidate's qualities, passion for their work and integrity? Would you eliminate them from your candidate pool if they described themselves as Velveeta? Focus on asking measurable questions in your interview and truly listen to your candidates. It is the best way to get the relevant information that you need. Anything else is, well ... cheesy!

Power Thought

Question your questions. Make sure they are relevant.

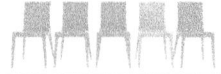

When interviewing for various positions within your organization, the real question you are often asking is, "Does this person have integrity?" The interview process between an administrative assistant and executive director is exactly the same. I have assisted my clients with interviewing for both positions using the same set of initial questions in order to truly determine this first critical job requirement.

A *good* employee will be dependable and consistent, fulfilling their commitments to the position. A *great* employee will also have your back; when you need to have a task accomplished in your business, you can count on that person to get it done. This "integrity philosophy" is the basis for A-list Interviews 91 percent success rate when placing a candidate. While the skillsets of positions within your company may be vastly different, one thing remains the same: the candidate that is hired is the one that will do the job to the best of their ability and beyond.

Power Thought

Hire great employees and
they will make your company great.

Peter Drucker says that two-thirds of all hiring decisions are found to be a mistake within that first year. Dr. Pierre Mornell says that if you rectify the situation of a bad hire within six months, then it will cost you 2 ½ times that person's annual salary. The cost of a bad hire is staggering! And I'm convinced this is a contributing reason to any economic recession.

Could an improved interview process help businesses succeed? Of course! As a matter of fact, if you want to get serious about your business, then you need to get serious about interviewing effectively. I recently helped the manager of a small retail store by teaching the person how to interview effectively. Together, we hired seven people, including the front line, the marketing director, and the manager. Within 90 days, we saw a 96 percent drop in customer complaints, and all three revenue centers increased an average of 19 percent. Imagine what all companies could do if they revamped their interview process!

Power Thought
The best and brightest in business are those willing to learn and pivot.

I was recently conducting an interview for one of my clients. As I introduced myself to a well-dressed candidate, the first question she asked was, "What animal left the long green poop on the sidewalk? Was it a goose? I think it's a goose."

While the question was entertaining, the inappropriateness of the comment showed that this candidate was not thinking about the interview at hand. Listening to the random comments of your future employee will give you amazing insight into whether they are really interested in *this* job, not just *a* job. Look for people who are focused on the job you are offering and who present themselves in the best possible light to ensure they will receive this job offer. If poop is their first question, probably not the A-list candidate you are looking for ☺.

Power Thought

If your head and your gut are battling over a decision, take
time to figure out why there is a conflict.
When your head and gut are in alignment,
you'll be sure to make the right decision.

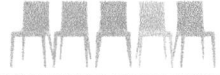

My passion for interviewing for A-list candidates was born from a horrible hiring mistake that I made. My first business required that I hire a manager to help run the day-to-day activities. I chose the wrong person and the mistake almost cost me my business.

I began to search for people who could really teach me how to interview for the best people. I was shocked to learn that interviewing techniques are really not taught in our business schools! Not one of the top ten MBA programs in the country has a dedicated class on how to effectively select top talent. I then began to think that the question should be, "*How* do we teach interviewing?" Here's why that's the right question: The most effective way to teach interviewing is in the room *with* the hiring manager and the candidate. I can speak to the intricacies and subtleties of interviewing, but it doesn't sink in until you see it, practice it and then integrate it into your own style.

The industry likes to discuss traditional versus behavioral interviewing techniques to screen for the best candidates. My argument with these techniques is that, at best, these styles are only 55 percent accurate in measuring for the best candidate. And rarely do you find a provider who properly teaches the technique. Sure you can find the information in a book, but the nuances that people bring to the table when interviewing are so vast that reading the material in a book will only get you half way to your goal. There are also a few classes in the marketplace that can give you some of the basics around effective interviewing, but nothing replaces hands-on learning.

When someone tells you that they teach interviewing skills, the first question should be "How?" The next question should be "Are you in the room with me when I am interviewing?" Invest in your business by truly learning how to find the A-list candidates that fit into your culture and who have the level of integrity needed to truly shine for your company.

Power Thought

The most insightful questions are actually not questions.
"Tell me about XYZ" is much more effective at
soliciting information.

I have been asked by hiring managers and recruiters about my active-to-passive-ratio. This ratio reflects the number of people interviewed who are currently unemployed versus employed. An active candidate is currently unemployed and actively looking for a position. A passive candidate is currently employed, relatively satisfied with their current position and may or may not be interested in a new position. My question to those who hire was, "Why is that important?"

Some employers are specifically *not* hiring people because they are unemployed. They believe that all unemployed people are unqualified candidates. The thought process is that if this person lost their job, then they must have been underperforming. As a hiring specialist, I see an amazing number of qualified applicants in both categories. According to the Bureau of Labor Statistics, over two million people quit their jobs in April 2010, the highest number in over a year. Are they also unqualified? Judging an entire group of people based on one qualification is called a bias or a prejudice; not only is it wrong, but it simply misses the whole point. You can't judge a book by its cover, and you can't judge a person's effectiveness by their employment status.

Power Thought

Look past the obvious bias to see the potential.

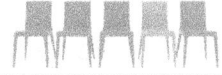

Have you ever walked by a small dust bunny on the floor and thought, *I should sweep that up*? Instead, you lift the corner of the rug and shove it underneath with your toe. Later, you take time to lift up the rug and are appalled by what you find!

Hiring for a vacant position works much the same way. Before starting the interview process, take time to evaluate and "sweep up" your job position so you can start your search from a fresh perspective. Review the job description with the person who is exiting. Revisit how the open position fits into the company structure and make changes to its reporting requirements. Reinvent the duties, responsibilities, and expectations of the position to meet any progressive changes within the company. Then, shake out the rug by letting go of any residual bad feelings you may have about the previous employee, especially if the termination was unpleasant.

Cleaning your rug and sprucing up the position is not only a necessary thing to do for the company, but it sets up your A-list Candidate for a successful working experience.

Power Thought

Spring cleaning does wonders for your house, and cleaning up your job description will do the same for your company.

When I'm first hired, I've had countless clients tell me, "Beth, you should have seen this person in the interview! They were amazing! And then I had to fire them two weeks later. What did I miss?" The answer to this burning question is that many hiring managers and executives *do not* realize the power of the interviewer.

When interviewing a candidate, it is important to remember that you are in charge of the *entire* experience. Usually, the interviewer controls the time of the interview, the date, the day of the week, the location, the agenda, the questions, the structure, the process, who is on the team, the outcome of the decision to hire and whether or not the candidate will ever find out if they got the job. In all aspects, the interviewer is in total control *… and the candidate knows it.*

This type of "power" over another adult rarely occurs in our society, and when it does, there is usually extreme violence involved. Most of us are not exposed to this type of control, so we don't realize this dynamic in an interview. How can we? We have no experience with it. This means that the candidate, who is nervous, anxious, worried and vulnerable, will do whatever it takes in order to please the interviewer and secure the position. Once the candidate gets the job, this power difference is dramatically reduced. The new employee becomes comfortable and relaxed in their work environment, becoming their true selves, sometimes with disastrous results.

Because I interview as a profession, I understand this dynamic. I teach my clients about this power difference and what they can do to reduce it. For example, before the interview I inform the candidate of the agenda for the interview. I give the person options for interviewing times. When they show up 15 minutes early, I am ready to begin their interview 15 minutes early. I have their resume and cover letter in front of me for reference, but my real purpose is to actively listen to what they have to say. At the end of each interview I inform the candidate as to when they can expect to hear from us. I then follow through as promised. I do not withhold information from my candidates, especially when the answer is "no."

In order to see your candidate's true selves and determine if they are the amazing employee you are seeking, give some power back to the person during the interview process. Treat each individual with the respect and dignity they deserve, and they in kind will perform when hired.

Power Thought

You can't hire effectively without candidates coming to interviews. Make sure that you treat them well during the interview process.

© Randy Glasbergen
www.glasbergen.com

GLASBERGEN

"My short-term goal is to bluff my way through this job interview. My long-term goal is to invent a time machine so I can come back and change everything I've said so far."

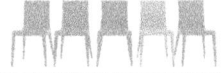

In looking back on the most recent Great Recession, it is good to learn from our mistakes. One of the biggest mistakes made in business is the blatant disregard for a professionally run interview process. We spend so much time, energy and money trying to replace the actual interviews. We use recruiters, phone interviews, and employee testing just so we don't have to interview candidates. But, guess what? You can *never* avoid the actual interview.

Even if you decide to hire someone without having met the person, you still have to speak to the candidate and perform that initial interview. You can't avoid it. So, how do we fix this? Simply by talking about the big white elephant in the room, and acknowledging what Martin Yates calls a "dirty secret."

Companies promote people to management, tell them to hire a team of people, hold them accountable for that team, and never teach them how to conduct an effective interview. When someone makes a big hiring mistake, they falsely assume, "I'm just not good at interviewing." That isn't true! People can be taught to conduct fast, effective interviews. However, until we begin talking about it, the interview process will remain in the dark. And company cultures will continue to deteriorate.

Power Thought

Don't avoid the interview ...
learn how to conduct an effective one.

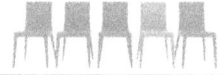

Occasionally, my clients are faced with a decision to re-hire a former employee. People may leave an organization for any number of reasons: more money, different opportunities and loss of passion for a position are common ones. I was asked for my opinion by a client who wanted to re-hire a former employee. My honest answer: "Well, it depends."

Re-hiring a former employee can have some advantages. Training and ramp up speed are often reduced. But there can also be some disadvantages, like wasting valuable resources on an employee who is not really engaged with you or your business. Following a few guidelines can help in your decision-making process:

1. *Did your re-hire "leave well"?* Did this person give you notice and wrap up projects before their departure? Did they leave on good terms and help with creating a job description or training their replacement? Remember that the manner in which your employee left you the first time will be the way they leave you the second time.

2. *Will your re-hire add value to your current culture?* Chances are your business has changed since your employee has left. Make sure this person is still a fit for your business and the position.

3. *Realize that it may be short term.* If your re-hire left once, it is most likely because certain needs were not being met. Will those needs be met now? What has changed since their last period of employment with you? Make sure that you both address any un-met needs—on both sides—before bringing someone back on board.

One of my former colleagues in the restaurant industry often had kitchen staff that would periodically leave for more money, less hours, etc. He always thanked them for their service and let them pursue the new opportunity. Invariably, they would realize that life was not always greener on the other side of the fence and would try to come back. The ones that left with integrity and honesty were hired back immediately. Those who left poorly, were not hired back.

Should you re-hire an employee? Only if that decision supports your efforts as the company leader. If hiring that person creates more hardship, why bother?

Power Thought

Graciousness and integrity are hallmarks of exemplary people. It is good to re-hire employees that have "learned by leaving" that you are a great employer!

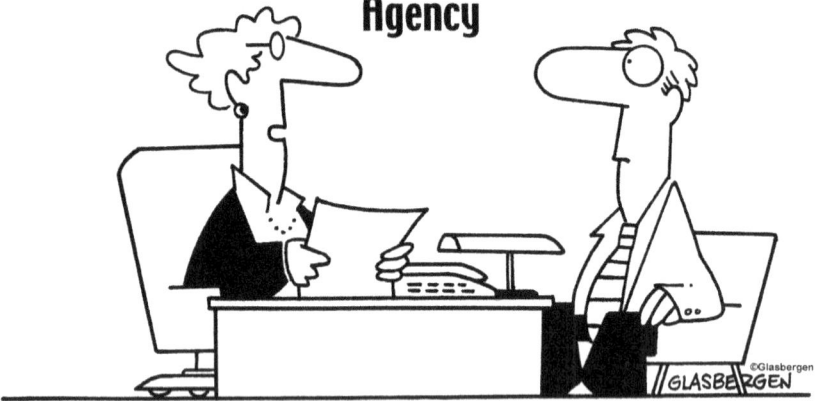

Collection Agency

"Before I can hire you, you'll have to take a blood test. We're looking for people with ice water in their veins."

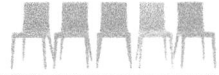

Every once in a while, I apply for jobs just to see what candidates have to go through in order to get a position. It is important as an interviewer to understand the process from the candidate's perspective; the application process is a direct reflection of the company who is hiring. While every interview process is different, if you want to *not* hire good people, here are some to-do's:

1. *Make the application process so hard that good candidates would rather have a root canal.* One company I applied for posted an ad with an incorrect link. I was curious about the position so I went to the company website and located the right link. I discovered that I had to write an essay of my qualifications and how they fit into the job description. I also had to send a resume, cover letter, references, and a salary history. The link to send the materials was also incorrect so I moved on to the next one. While gathering good information on your candidates is important, asking for too much will discourage the applicant and give you more paperwork to review. A well-crafted resume and cover letter should tell you all that you need to know to determine if you should move to the next step in the interview process.

2. *Be disrespectful of the candidate's time.* One company asked to schedule an interview with me, and asked me to be 20 minutes early. The day before the interview, I received a frantic email asking me to arrive another 40 minutes earlier. I was an hour early as requested, however, the interview started at the original time.

3. *Leave people hanging.* I interviewed with another company that told me they would give me an answer within three days. Two weeks went by without any communication. I sent a follow up email re-iterating my interest in the position, and I still had not heard from them. If you do not intend to hire the candidate, at least send them an email thanking them for applying and let them know you filled the position.

4. *Be confusing.* One company asked me to interview and I ended up watching a 45-minute sales presentation. This is not an interview!

5. *Be vague.* A company that doesn't put their name on the job ad will get people looking for a job. A company that stands behind their ad with their name on it will get people looking for the next perfect position.

Power Thought

How are you treating your candidates?
Is your process respectful of them or not?

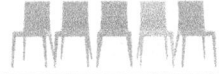

I recently asked my network on LinkedIn how we can improve the relationship between job candidates and the organizations that conduct the interviews. I was stunned at the response. Every respondent replied with a request to *communicate more effectively*. One person stated, "While I don't want the answer to be no ... let me get you off my list!"

A-list Interviews responds to every application we receive on behalf of our clients. Taking care of your candidates, even after the application process is completed, is a direct reflection of your company, not to mention an incredible marketing opportunity. While I agree that some respondents do not take the news of rejection well, the incredible people who are ideal for another company deserve the respect of a response. It is as easy as an auto responder email stating, "Thank you for your application. If you haven't heard from us by x date, then we have moved on with other candidates."

In closing, when you post an ad, get some free marketing by responding to your applicants and Just Say No!

Power Thought

Those who are thoughtful are thought well of by others.

My clients and I were interviewing a man who arrived prepared with several sealed 8x11 envelopes. When he sat down, he asked if we needed a copy of his resume. I said, "No thank you" because I already had one sitting on the table in front of me that he had provided. He mentioned that he also brought some additional documents such as references. I was concerned when he began describing his last manager with anger and venom, and decided I wanted to see his references. When he struggled with the envelope's seal, I wondered why the envelopes were sealed to begin with, then he whipped out a huge serrated edge knife to slice one open. Wide eyed in amazement, we unfortunately did not hear what he said because we were so focused on that knife. We ended the interview quickly, realizing that the candidate was probably not a great fit. While this individual had some really amazing experience, my client actually felt threatened in the interview process.

Be careful how you present yourself to future employers. While opening a letter with an appropriate tool is certainly understandable, carrying a weapon into the interview is probably not the best way to secure your chances for employment.

Power Thought

If you feel threatened by a candidate in the interview
process, don't ignore that feeling!

Christopher Robin: "There now. Did I get your tail back on properly, Eeyore?"

Eeyore: "No matter. I'll most likely lose it again anyway."

Last month, I interviewed a candidate who was world weary, tired and unhappy. This person had been out of work for a long time in an industry that is rapidly changing. The overall impact was the "Eeyore Effect."

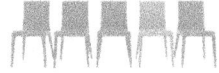

Christopher Robin and his gang are forever reaching out to help their friend re-attach his tail, but Eeyore shows no appreciation for their efforts. Not only does he *not* thank Christopher Robin for helping him, he criticizes Christopher's work. He also puts forth no effort to permanently find a solution to his tail falling off. Has he thought about super glue? Stitches? Duct tape? In other words, Eeyore is an energy drainer. He is hard to be around. He has very little enthusiasm for his life, his work, his tail or even his friends. Can you imagine as if you had an employee like this?

Watch for the "Eeyore Effect" while you are interviewing, even when faced with the world weary, tired and unhappy. (Thanks to Michelle Barnes for "The Eeyore Effect.")

Power Thought

"Do not grow weary in well doing" is a good motto to follow.

You may not be aware that before I became an interviewing specialist, I owned and managed a restaurant in Boulder, Colorado. When I owned the restaurant, I hired a manager who committed several crimes right under my nose. I really had no idea how bad it was until my two best managers turned in their notices together. They sat me down and told me horror stories about what it was like to work at my place of business, and ultimately mine and my family's second home. We fired the thieving manager immediately. After the fired manager was gone, the complaints started pouring in; my employees suddenly felt they could freely speak about this former employee. We had lost really good staff and continued to have turn over as a result of this incident.

If it were not for the courage of these two managers, who at the time were ready to quit, I still would not have known what was going on in my business. I had heard complaints before from other staff members, but I didn't take them seriously. Looking back on it, I should have. Why didn't I? Because the complaints seemed so minor. "He didn't do his side work right." "He didn't wipe down the counters." "He makes me do his work for him, even though he pays me for it." I thought people were just blowing off steam.

After I fired him, I asked my staff, "Why didn't you tell me that he was stealing money/inventory/food?"

The answer was always the same: "Beth, I tried to talk to you about this."

The biggest complaints that I hear from my clients is that they wish their employees would be more forthcoming about problems in the business/department. But, the employees say, "If you don't take my small problems seriously, how am I supposed to talk to you about the big stuff?" In other words, those early, seemingly minor, complaints are opportunities for employees to see how you handle the little stuff. They are trying to figure out if you will hear them with the big stuff. They will talk to you about the tip of the iceberg as a way to begin the conversation about the bottom of the iceberg.

Your job as the boss is to take complaints very seriously, even the smallest of them. Usually, if you have an employee who is willing to talk to you, the problem is bigger than they indicate. Use this opportunity to take a good look at the work environment you are providing and make sure it is operating the way that you intend. Don't ignore it, or you will be "the last to know."

Power Thought

Being quick to hear and quick to understand are good
skills imperative to being seen as a great boss!

I met with a potential client that needed to hire several new employees for his business expansion. As I was learning his goals, he told me, "The war on talent is killing my business. There aren't enough talented people for the positions out there." His frustration was obvious.

His comment made me think about this often cited "War on Talent." What does it really mean? Does it truly exist? The phrase "War on Talent" can conjure up images of war when discussing recruiting efforts, and is enough to cause gut-wrenching fear in my clients in an area of business that is already met with trepidation and cynicism. Utter these three little words, and my strong, competitive, innovative, wildly successful business leaders are suddenly reduced to panic mode, believing it will be a bitter fight to find great employees.

To be clear, the word "War" itself is inflammatory and emotionally charged. It is also wildly inaccurate when it comes to recruitment efforts. You do not hear news about Sergey from Google and Mark from Facebook whipping out their swords and dueling over a potential employee. They may be negotiating an offer, or determining an attractive salary and benefits package to woo an ideal candidate, but no one is actually "at war." This exercise in attracting good employees is hardly enough to have my clients in crisis, who negotiate contracts daily within the course of their businesses.

In this so called "War on Talent," I ask who exactly is the enemy? Other companies? The actual candidate? Who are we fighting exactly? The word "Talent" is also incredibly misleading. "Talented" (better described as experienced) for one position is not necessarily considered talented for another position. In the book *Talent Is Overrated: What REALLY Separates World-Class Performers from Everyone Else,* researchers from the INSEAD business school in France and the US Naval Postgraduate School call the phenomenon of looking for talented people as "the experience trap." Their key finding was that while companies typically value experienced managers over less experienced personnel, rigorous studies show that, on average, "managers with experience didn't produce high caliber outcomes."' So then "talent" is not really "talent." A high-producing employee can be hired, trained and cultivated, regardless of "talent."

In addition, the misnomer to this expression is further exacerbated by the fact that it was created in 1997, when Steven Hankin of McKinsey & Co popularized the phrase in their report and accompanying book. There are two billion more people on this planet than there were in 1997, yet the current employee landscape is referenced to a 20 plus years old phrase—and mindset! After breaking it down, we think there is a war over potential employees because we are focused on talent. The reality is we have a broken recruiting process that prevents good candidates from consideration for positions where they could perform well and even excel. The current broken process starts the minute a job becomes available with the employer. This outdated process keeps us from finding and recognizing the right people for our teams. Here is a break down using a 7-step process to interviewing:

Step 1: *Create an Ideal Candidate List.* The recruiting process begins with the recognition that you need more people to get a job done and get the job done right and/or a vacancy within a current position. This is where we must begin to shift our thinking from a *war* mentality to a *discovery* mentality. Before we do anything else, we must define what we are looking for in the ideal candidate. What type of person is needed for this position? What attributes must this person have to be successful in this role? Most companies overlook this first step, the first big mistake.

You cannot find the person you want for a position unless you know what you want in that person. If you need a person with tenacity to discover new research, then hiring someone without that trait will not help you. Define your ideal candidate, down to quirks, traits and personality type, then hold out until you find that person. Create the vision and stick to it!

Step 2: *Write a job description.* I get the most complaints about this part of the process. "Do I *really* have to write a job description, Beth?" Yes, yes you do. How else will you make sure that your new employee gets trained properly on the tasks at hand? Also, it helps to communicate with the new employee on how to be successful in the role. The job description is the most essential component to your action plan *after* the person is hired. Do not skimp on this step!

Step 3: *Write a job ad.* Your job ad is vastly different from the job description. This document is an invitation for potential employees to apply for their dream job. Begin the ad with your company mission statement to attract like-minded people. You want applicants who pursue this job and this company, because this is the job they want.

Step 4: *Do not make it hard for candidates to apply.* In its job application process, there was a college that wanted to hire a career counselor, and required the candidates to write a three-to-five-page paper on the history of the school. While a writing sample and comprehension skills may be essential, someone must read those five-page papers, evaluate them, and determine acceptability. Plus, what potential candidate is going to write a five-page paper before they get a job without grumbling? *They need a job.* They want to apply, be notified of an interview (or not) and happily write perhaps a one-page paper to share skill level. Yet many organizations make it hard to get candidates through the interviewing process as a guise of screening to reduce candidates. You need more people to interview rather than fewer, especially in a competitive employment situation.

Step 5: *Use your Applicant Tracking System wisely.* An applicant tracking system is designed to make sure that applicants are not lost in the process. It should not be used to weed out applicants. The biggest complaint that I hear from your future employees is that no one is even looking at their application. They feel like they are weeded out based on a computer algorithm ... and they are right. Instead, use your applicant tracking systems to weed people *in*, instead of weeding them out, by adding a human touch to the initial selection process.

Step 6: *You are a customer service representative.* Respond to applicants like you would your clients. Be proactive, be courteous and be forthcoming with information. Let them know if they did not get the job or even if they will not be interviewing for the job. You can easily send out emails to candidates who are not moving forward in the process. This is honorable, and because other companies don't respond to candidates, you put yourself in a position to get more candidates for jobs in the future. In other words, this is marketing for your company.

Step7: *Change your mindset from fear to abundance.* Hiring a new person is an exciting time! It means that your company is stable and growing. When you hire from a place of fear, you prevent yourself from being able to find the right fit. Shift your mindset from fear to excitement and you'll see what a difference that makes! There is no war when it comes to finding great people. This gut-wrenching fear that you have over not being able to have the right people join your company is just that: irrational fear that is made up. Let go of this debilitating mindset by adjusting your recruiting process to reflect a more current landscape of the employee experience. ☺

Power Thought

FEAR is False Evidence Appearing Real ... Let go of what is
false and hold on to what is real.

"We're looking for someone who can stretch
with the demands of this job. Are you flexible?"

I have had several business owners and hiring managers ask me about why candidates are "ghosting" them for interviews. In case you are not familiar with the term, ghosting means "the practice of ending a personal relationship with someone by suddenly, and without explanation, withdrawing from all communication." Apparently, candidates are ghosting potential employers with increased frequency. The job seeker applies for a job and when the company calls them for an interview, the candidate either never responds or schedules the interview and then never shows up. Several employers that I have discussed this issue with are really upset and rightly so, especially when the candidate schedules and does not show up for the interview. If you are encountering this issue, here are a few suggestions:

- *Most importantly, take a big deep breath.* If a candidate does not show up for an interview, you now have 30 minutes to an hour to get something else done that you may not have had time to accomplish in your day. The candidate did you a huge favor by not attending the interview. No call/no show behavior would have most likely appeared in their job performance, if they had made it through the hiring process and began working for you. Be grateful; they just made your job easier by not having to fire them later.

- *Don't take it personally.* I am seeing ghosting from *all* levels of candidates, from entry level to senior level and in all industries. It is not happening to just you and your organization. Remember, employers are the ones who first started ghosting when they quit responding to *all* candidate inquiries. A simple "thanks but no thanks" is all recruits want when they apply and are not chosen. As hiring professionals, it is hard to justify being too upset now that the tables have turned when non-responsiveness to candidates has been commonplace.

- *Turn the opportunity into a positive learning experience.* Remember that candidates also deserve your best customer service. Return messages, calls and emails in a timely fashion. Be courteous and do what you say you are going to do when you set expectations with your potential hires. You cannot eliminate all ghosting from candidates, but you can do your part to create a great place to work.

Power Thought

Be a great host.
Don't ghost.

In the movie "Up in the Air," George Clooney remarks "I stereotype. It's faster." It may be faster, but it is not 100 percent predictable; you cannot predict an employee's success in their position by stereotyping. I work with business owners and hiring managers every day who use stereotypes to predict their employees' success or failure. I say that for every stereotype that exists and is used to predict behavior, I have a success story to disprove it.

One stereotype is that unemployed people are lazy so they are often overlooked. This is not always the case. In 2008, many people became unemployed, due to the Recession, but afterwards there was an influx of new small businesses. Those same people who could have been stereotyped as being "lazy" or "unmotivated" came out of the recession and created jobs for themselves and others; I predict this will be the same outcome after the Covid-19 chaos subsides. Are some unemployed people lazy? Yes. Are some employed people lazy? Yes. Does employment status correlate directly with work ethic? No.

One time I interviewed a gentleman who had been unemployed for six months because his company had gone out of business. When I asked him to interview, he said that he could come in whenever I wanted him to. When I asked him about vacation time, he replied, "I'm sick of vacation. I've repainted the house. I've cleaned out the garage. I've remodeled the basement. I've refurbished old furniture and I've replanted the garden. I'm ready to go back to work." Does he sound lazy to you?

Which interview method works best to accurately predict the likelihood of success for an employee? The answer may surprise you. It isn't stereotyping. In fact, all you have to do is listen. Don't talk. Don't think about the next question you are going to ask. Don't look at your phone. Don't clean your fingernails. Don't tie your shoes. Sit. Focus. Listen. Really *hear*, *observe*, and *absorb* what your candidate is telling you. Be entirely present to the moment, and the candidate will let you know if they will be successful.

Power Thought

Distraction is the enemy of insight,
understanding, and progress.

I have seen companies post a blind ad—an ad posted without using the company name—as their first step in their search for a new employee. Ads with the same job title and similar job descriptions don't stand out to candidates without the company name because without a name, companies are virtually indistinguishable from one another. The ad sets the tone for the application process, so generic ads bring in generic applicants.

You don't want your open position to be "run of the mill" because you don't want your candidate to be from that same mill. To find someone who is passionate, proud of their work, and eager to better themselves and your company, you must showcase those same attributes in your ad.

Including your company name says, "Please apply, quality candidates, come join our team." It advertises that your company is eager to find someone, just as they should be eager to find you. The perfect candidate for your company won't blend in with the crowd, so don't allow your ad to do that either; post an ad that will bring in candidates who don't just want a job, but who want *your* job.

Power Thought

Honesty and transparency are hallmarks of great
companies ... and great people.

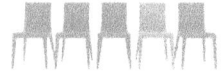

Many people are confused about the role of an interviewer. Some people think that an interviewer is a Human Resources professional. Human resources is defined as the function within an organization charged with managing policies related to the management of individuals who already work in the establishment. The responsibility interviewers perform is the formal meetings for the assessment of the qualifications of an applicant; interviewers identify future staff. While the roles of human resource professionals sometimes require them to also perform the duties of an interviewer, this is not essentially part of their job description.

People also often confuse interviewers with recruiters or headhunters. Recruiters solicit people to apply for positions. Interviewers select the candidates and determine the finalists for review by management of the company. If your human resources department is performing interviews, look into additional training to give them the appropriate tools. Nowhere in their education is this job skill addressed, and no one can replace the hiring manager in the interview process.

Power Thought

No one can be an expert in everything; therefore, training
is essential for success.

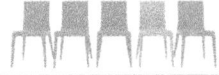

One of the things we value the most is trust. We look for trust in friendships and relationships and often depend on it in business. In professional settings it's more likely referred to as confidentiality but regardless, the idea remains the same: trust is part of the foundation of all relationships and without it, progress and growth are less likely. If you can't trust your employees to keep certain things confidential, what *can* you trust them to do?

I once interviewed a candidate who disclosed that their current boss was going through bankruptcy. The candidate supplied us with their employer's name, address, and telephone number. While this seemed rather inappropriate, an even bigger offense is the fact that the candidate worked in a financial industry and had licenses that prevented him by law from disclosing someone else's financial situation. When I pointed this out, my client said, "So we can't trust that this candidate won't talk about our clients' financial situations."

My client was right. Disparaging a former boss or co-worker is a red flag in any interview process, no matter what industry or position. Discussing information that is protected by law is not only illegal, it is unethical. If you are interviewing anyone who reveals too much information about their current or former company, they are not the person for you. If they willingly gossip *to* you, then they'd have no qualms gossiping *about* you.

Power Thought

"The act of slaying another's reputation is moral suicide."
~ Neville Goddard

What you see in an interview is what you get ... kind of. During an interview, most candidates try to put their best foot forward so if anything is less than impressive, that quality will only be magnified when they relax and settle into the new job. Whatever you ignore in the interview will likely be the reason you consider firing the person down the road.

I recently interviewed a candidate who was seemingly perfect for our position on paper. He had the skills, the education, the experience—everything we could hope for. During the interview however, he completely missed the mark. This candidate sat across from me with his seat pushed back from the table and a foot on the seat of the chair. He then proceeded to tell me that his current boss was "annoying, but it is probably because I slept with her." The inappropriate disclosure of his sexual activities coupled with overly casual body language was more than enough to tell me he was not our guy.

When candidates come in and present obvious red flags, don't disregard those flags because the person looks good on paper. No matter how skilled, educated, or experienced someone is, they aren't your dream hire if they aren't respectful, verbally and physically, in the interview.

Power Thought

Your body is always talking even when
you aren't saying a word.

When an entrepreneur needs to hire for a position, they often rely on what I call "The Friends & Family Plan" when hiring new staff. One client even confessed that he would call his friends to find out who needed a job and determine how quickly they could start. While he readily admitted this process was ineffective, he simply did not know how else to hire.

As your business grows, it is critical to evolve past the mindset that just because you know that person, it does not mean they will work well with you or your company. While the modicum of trust may ease your mind temporarily, this path often leads to a mis-hire, decreased productivity, and a destroyed friendship. Can you imagine how awkward Thanksgiving would be if you had to fire your brother-in-law for not doing his job? Learning and practicing a well-defined interview process in lieu of a friends and family search will get you more qualified employees and save a few relationships along the way.

Power Thought

The Friends and Family Plan works for cell phones,
not for hiring.

There are plenty of situations where flirting is appropriate: while waiting in line for coffee, shopping for groceries, or walking through the park. However, the interview process is *not* one of them. Not only is it inappropriate, it is a major red flag and will most likely lead to further uncomfortable sexual behavior that you do not want brought into your company.

Last summer, I was knee-deep in the interviewing process for one of my clients. We had been through several candidates, looking for the perfect A-list player for their team. The last interview of the day looked incredibly promising! The woman who sat across from us was qualified, both technically and culturally. As the candidate began asking her questions, she leaned over and winked at my client! During a different interview, another candidate leaned over to my client and said, "You're so much more beautiful in person than in your photos."

These flirtatious actions do not fit in with the professionalism expected in an interview. If you as the employer are uncomfortable in the interview, then you will really be uncomfortable when the individual is on your payroll, no matter how "qualified" they are.

Power Thought

Ulterior motives will sink a career or business—fast.

Barbara Walters and I Have the Same Job Title, but not the Same Job.

Barbara Walters is one of the best interviewers in the world. She is prepared, she does her research, and people tell her things they don't tell anyone else. She asks probing questions, and is amazing at letting the conversation take its course.

I am also an interviewer, but my job is vastly different from Ms. Walters for one reason: The power difference between the interviewer and a candidate is one-sided for the interviewer. Barbara Walters is a powerhouse in her own right, yet the people who she interviews run countries. There isn't a large power difference on her side. They aren't looking to her to provide them a livelihood, and really, she looks to them for her livelihood.

When a hiring manager is interviewing, they typically don't understand the enormous power they have over their candidates; when you don't understand the dynamic between two people, you can't make effective hiring decisions. Interviewing is one of the rare instances where power is completely one-sided. The interviewer holds the fate of the candidate in their hands because usually the interviewee has no idea what the interviewer is looking for. Keep in mind how nervous, anxious, and afraid your candidates might be so that you can have a better understanding of who they are and who they would be as an employee.

Power Thought

Give someone a measure of power and
you will see their true character come out.

39

"Powell's Rules for Picking People: Look for intelligence and judgment and, most critically, a capacity to anticipate, to see around corners. Also look for loyalty, integrity, a high energy drive, a balanced ego and the drive to get things done." ~ Colin Powell

In theory, this sounds like amazing advice. Focus on the person's attributes as opposed to their experience and you will find a great employee. But in practice, how can you tell in a 15-minute interview if a person has integrity? This is the age-old question that keeps great leaders up at night, worrying they may not have selected the right people. In a well-defined strategic interview, integrity, drive and loyalty are fairly easy to spot. Integrity is defined as, "Doing what you say you are going to do, when you say you are going to do it." Here are four ways to determine if your candidate has it:

1. *Following the directions set forth in the ad.* If you ask for a cover letter, a resume and the job title in the subject line, then only interview those who followed all of the directions. If they don't follow directions in the interview process, they won't do it once they have direct deposit. The stakes aren't nearly as high once they get the job.

2. *Meeting Deadlines.* An interview is not only the opportunity for a candidate to shine, but it is also a deadline that you can use to measure integrity. Did they show up on time? Are they prepared? Did they do research on the company? If not, then the chances of them being prepared once they get the job are low. Again, the stakes aren't nearly as high, once they get the job.

3. *Homework Assignments.* I was once in a position where a client really wanted to hire a person that I didn't want him to hire. We agreed to give this candidate a homework assignment and a third interview to see how well she performed. She blew it. Her assignment had spelling errors, grammar errors, wrinkled paper, and wrong information. Her energy level was low at the third interview, and she had little enthusiasm for the task at hand. She clearly did not want the job, and she showed no integrity towards the assignment.

4. *Look for Follow Up.* I am truly surprised at how rare it is to hear a candidate say "I really want this job. What do I have to do to get it?" A simple thank you email works really well to determine a person's drive and desire for a position. With all of the information available about how to *wow* hiring managers, many people simply don't, especially for a position that is not a good fit on some level. Do not ignore the signs that a candidate doesn't want the job, even if they are perfectly qualified.

At A-list Interviews, our entire Response Analysis System is specifically designed to screen candidates based on integrity with 91 percent retention rate after a year. Colin Powell is on to something. Let us teach you what it is.

Power Thought

Following proven rules of interviewing will give you confidence in the process and lead you to the best candidate for your company.

As I sat at the interviewing table looking out the window, a driver in a brand-new pickup truck came squealing into the parking lot, veered into a parking spot and slammed on his brakes. He threw open his door, climbed down from the truck and dropped his pants. He was wearing boxers and an undershirt. He removed a collared, button down shirt from a package, threw it over his shoulders, and proceeded to tuck it in, not knowing that he had an audience. As he ran in the door, apologizing that he was late, I realized this gentleman was our interviewee. He continued to button his shirt throughout the interview. When he looked out the window and realized that we had seen his entire performance, including his undergarments, he stayed for five minutes, then declared that he was no longer interested in this job and left.

We can appreciate that he came to the interview to let us know his thoughts on the job. He didn't just blow off the interview, which shockingly happens a lot. While he at least made an appearance, I doubt it was the appearance he intended. When examining candidates for your open job position, watch for clues in their behavior that will tell you the type of employee you will be hiring. This gentleman was a good example of someone who may struggle with organization, time keeping and professional appearance.

Power Thought

First impressions can be lasting impressions.

A client of mine and I were interviewing a few weeks ago, and a bright, savvy woman began telling us how this job was "beneath" her. Even though the job ad clearly stated the salary range, she then asked for a 20-30 percent increase. The salary conversation wasn't what lost her the job; this would have been easily negotiated if she had been passionate about the position.

What I find in my work as an interviewer is that candidates who really don't want the job being offered will spend a lot of time and energy focused on money and benefits. When someone applies for a job that they don't want, their motivation is likely monetary so that will be their primary concern. For the candidate that really wants the job, money is hardly ever the top priority, especially when the salary is clearly stated up front. When this very talented woman finds the job that she really wants, she will be dynamic, no doubt, and money won't be an issue for either side.

Power Thought

Money is a poor substitute for passion about the work.

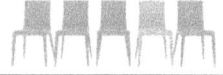

If you have read a women's magazine, there always seems to be an article about lying in a relationship. "Little white lies" can often seem harmless enough, but isn't this really a measurement for integrity and personal responsibility? I've often heard from my clients that they are appalled when a candidate exaggerates on their resume. Candidates are advised to be truthful and honest in their representation of themselves.

What happens when a company is lying to the candidate? According to the Reader's Digest article *Get Hired, Not Fired: 50 Secrets That Your HR Person Won't Tell You* company personnel are lying to candidates as well. For example, here are two excerpts from the Reader's Digest article:

"Background checks are expensive. Sometimes we bluff, get you the fill out the form and don't run it," states Cynthia Shapiro, former human resource executive and author.[1]

[1]"Sometimes, we'll tell you we ended up hiring someone internally—even if we didn't—just to get you off our backs." HR rep at a Fortune 500 Financial services Firm.[2]

At the end of the day, if lying is a standard practice in your company, you will not be able to hire good people and expect them to stay. Run a strategic, well defined interview process. Be upfront and completely committed to a healthy environment for your employees based on truth telling. The rewards will far outweigh any benefit you may have received by lying to your people.

Power Thought

Lying is like a cancer that eats away the core of a company.

1, 2 – http://mploid.com/2011/get-hired-not-fired

Quit Focusing on Resumes and Just Interview!

As hiring managers, we spend more time analyzing resumes than we do interviewing candidates. Most applicants don't write their own resumes or cover letters. Therefore, we spend time "pre-screening" candidates based on something they didn't produce. Have you ever looked at a candidate's application and knew they were *the one*? Then, you talk to that person on the phone and know that they would never work out?

Trying to judge a person on a piece of paper they likely didn't produce is the biggest waste of time and energy. If the applicant followed directions specifically, has no spelling or grammar mistakes, and the tone of the resume is appealing—which will weed out about 70-80 percent of applicants—then schedule an interview. You will know so much more from an interview, then you can make a logical decision based on the candidate, not a piece of paper.

Power Thought

Seeing is believing and you need to see someone before you can truly believe them.

I previously recounted a story about "The Winker," an inappropriate event that occurred during one of my interviewing sessions. A female candidate had winked at my client during the interview process, making him feel very uncomfortable. Although the candidate was very qualified, we did not hire her because of the discomfort experienced by all who were involved.

Well you might not believe this, but I had another instance of a winker at the interview table! Not only did she wink at my client, but the top button of her blouse popped open! I cannot stress enough that an interview is not the time or the place for sexual overtures and "Janet Jackson" style uniform malfunctions.

As an interviewer and coach, I certainly see inappropriateness from both men and women. Remember, if you are the employer and uncomfortable in any way about a candidate, listen to your discomfort, regardless of how qualified the candidate may appear. This type of behavior in an interview could be a sign of things to come, including a sexual harassment suit.

Power Thought

Pay attention to your intuition—it's there for a reason.

I placed a call to a candidate to invite her in for an interview. The message said, "Please enjoy the music while your party is reached." Then, I heard the song "Take This Job and Shove It."

Need I say more?

Power Thought

No matter the format, every message you send out says something about who you are.

I was screening applicants for a position that requires a high level of attention to detail. Not long into the search, I received a beautifully formatted resume. The candidate had all of the skills that we wanted in a new employee! I opened the cover letter to learn more about this bright prospect. The opening sentence said, "I am responding to your add ... ." The question then becomes do I overlook one small spelling error that spell check would not have caught or do I pass up this well-qualified individual for a simple mistake.

When screening for a position that will require analysis and detailed reporting, one small mistake could cost a company thousands. The error of not proofreading made by this candidate stood out so magnificently that I had to pass up this person. So much of pre-screening can be subjective. When making the final call, compare the resume to all required skills, not just the technical set listed on the resume. I would definitely not "add" this individual to the team.

Power Thought

The devil is *always* in the details.

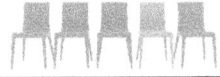

When my daughter Katy was five years old, she asked me if I believed in Santa Claus.

"Of Course!" I replied. "Why?"

She then said, "Really, Mom. Flying reindeer?"

Last month in the Denver Post, there was an article about a successful company trying to fill several open positions for their company. The woman interviewed commented, "On the first day, I was expecting 40 people to show up, one showed up ... I think now it is becoming almost easier to stay at home and accept an unemployment check than it is to get out there and work." First, I wondered how on earth this woman expected to interview 40 people in one day. That meant the candidates didn't have a specific time to come in for their interview. On my busiest day, I will interview 15 people, so logistically it simply doesn't make sense. Second, the myth that people sit back and milk unemployment benefits is simply not true. Now do we have folks in this country who scam the government for unemployment money? Of course. Do all of them? Of course not. Being unemployed is stressful; just ask anyone who has ever received unemployment. Third, I felt sympathetic towards this woman. She was overworked, overwhelmed, and doesn't believe there is help for her. What an awful position to be in as a business owner.

At A-list Interviews we begin with the ideal candidate in mind, so that every part of the process gets you closer to your best candidate. But you, as the owner or hiring manager, must believe the employee you want truly exists. When you believe, miracles can happen.

Power Thought

Your mind follows your belief system, so ask yourself,
"What do I really believe to be true?"

So you have a leaky faucet. It drips, drips, drips until eventually you have a corroded pipe and a higher water bill. Not investing in the development of your interview process can work in much the same way. The overall health of your company relies on capable people. The actual hiring of these people is a simple yes or no question. The real work of staffing begins with a strategic interview process and a well-trained interviewer. Without this, you may begin to erode the inner workings of your company.

If you want a strong, cohesive company, here are some good steps to follow:

- Describe the ideal person in detail.

- Create a new job description.

- Write your job description.

- Select and prep the interview team.

- Prepare a communication process that is respectful to candidates.

- Determine criteria for selecting the top candidate and define a system to communicate with those who were not chosen.

By approaching your new hire from a well-defined and strategic position, you will make better decisions and hire staff that will strengthen your company. Any process that skips these critical steps will simply corrode your company's "pipes." So do yourself a favor and avoid the drip, drip, drip.

Power Thought

Proactive is always better than reactive. Fix the drip.

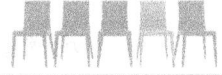

I recently talked to a client who said, "Just send me your top 5 people." Well, I can't, and here is why: No one can take the place of the hiring manager in the interview process. They know too much about the department or company, and their knowledge cannot be duplicated or ignored. However, the people I talk to would rather have a tooth pulled than conduct an interview. Why? Because they have *never* been trained. They view it, and rightly so, as a colossal waste of time because they are unprepared and the interviewing process is generally not done well. In his book *Hiring and Keeping the Best* Martin Yates calls interviewing "a dirty secret." We expect hiring managers to put a team of people together, we hold them accountable, then we are shocked when they aren't successful. If you want a team to be effective, you must concentrate your efforts on an effective interview process, including training the people who will be responsible for the hiring. Otherwise, just flip a coin and call it good.

Power Thought

Hiring and training are execrably linked together.

Why do employers ask candidates for salary histories? I did some research and found out there are a few reasons. 1) If a candidate is taking too large of a pay cut, then it might lead to job dissatisfaction. 2) Some employers think that steady increases in salary prove a candidate's competency. 3) Some employers want to see if a candidate is requesting the same salary range that the company is providing.

The facts are: 1) People take pay cuts all the time and are happier. Not all are dissatisfied. 2) Several studies have proven that money isn't always what motivates people. A steady increase in salary could prove a person's passion for one's job. 3) If you want to know what people are making, then get a more global sense of it by going to salary.com or a comparable website.

Here are my thoughts. A person's salary is confidential and private. To exclude a person from applying for a position because they won't disclose their salary is prejudicial, biased and short-sighted. To base a hiring decision on salary requirements may prevent you from finding an excellent employee.

Power Thought
Respecting privacy means you respect and value the individual.

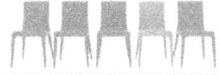

When I interview 14 people in a day and write two-to-three pages worth of notes on each, my fingers can get really stiff. I will bend them a few times and shake them out, causing my knuckles to pop occasionally.

Last week, in an interview with a hiring manager, I was in the middle of asking my questions and my fingers popped. The candidate sitting across from me reached over to hold my hand and shouted, "Don't pop your knuckles! Ewwww!"

I get that some people are offended by knuckle popping and I do my best to keep it to a minimum. This candidate, however, didn't even say please or thank you with her request, which was stated at the top of her lungs. If she is willing to yell at me in front of her potential boss, imagine what she might do to your customers.

Ewwww!

Power Thought

What people say or do spontaneously
gives insight into who they truly are.

Do Looks Matter in Interviewing?

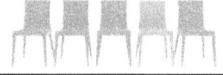

I ask my clients regularly about their thoughts on a candidate after the initial interview. Usually, I get responses like, "He had a stain on his shirt" and "Did you notice the scuff marks on her shoes?" While I realize that first impressions are often centered on a person's appearance, it may or may not be a factor in your hiring decision. I like to probe further and ask about their thoughts on the candidate's personality. After several "Umm's" and deer-in-the-headlight looks, they finally come up with comments such as, "They were a bit whiny" or "I'm not sure."

Let me give an example. I interviewed a candidate who complained about his boss, his co-workers in multiple jobs, his company, and his work. Nothing and no one seemed to make him happy. During our interview rap up, I asked the client, "So what did you think?"

"His tie was askew and his hair wasn't combed," she replied.

I questioned further and discovered that she wasn't impressed because she felt he was a whiner and would have difficulty working with him. The next candidate that we interviewed walked in well prepared. He presented a list of recommendations, asked well-researched questions and had a great attitude. He let us know that he had come to the business site three days before the interview to make sure he would not get lost on the day of his interview. He said, "Even if I don't get the job, I wanted to tell you my thoughts on how this could be improved."

After he left, I asked my clients, "What was he wearing?"

No one could remember. They didn't even remember that he wore glasses! We hired him and he is currently in his third year. The moral of this story is that when people are wowed by someone, their looks don't matter. But when faced with a personality flaw, we often describe it in terms of their appearance, i.e., "The Whiner had an askew tie."

When you are interviewing your candidates, remember to listen to their words and pay attention to their use of language and their preparedness. These qualities are much more indicative of their performance than their appearance.

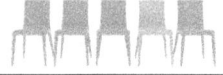

Like most consultants I know, my office is in various coffee shops along the Front Range of Colorado. As a result, I hear many different conversations. Last week, I was sitting next to two women in one of my favorite office locations. They were having a heated discussion about Woman #1's abrupt departure from Woman #2's company. The conversation went something like this:

Boss: "I can't believe that you left!"

Employee: "I told you why I was frustrated!"

Boss: "But I thought we fixed the scheduling problem. You didn't tell me about the other issues. I can't fix it if I don't know about it!"

Employee: "How can you not know about it? You are the boss!"

The "boss" is ultimately responsible for everything that happens within their company. One important responsibility is to ensure a healthy work environment for all employees. In this scenario, or any scenario for that matter, blaming an employee for lack of communication does not resolve the issue. I find most often that employees attempt to discuss problems in a very subtle way. They often feel hesitant to make complaints because they are really unsure of how receptive said boss will be. To help you spark the conversation with your employees, look for the signs that an employee is thinking about leaving:

- Your top performer is now underperforming. If you begin to have performance problems with someone that you've never had an issue with, it is time to ask them what's going on.

- Your employee asks about another opportunity in your company. This means they are not feeling challenged and have become bored with their current position and may be considering a change or they hate their current boss.

- Your employee mentions that another company is trying to recruit them. This is a very subtle way of an employee letting you know that they are exploring options.

If you don't want to be caught unaware, then listen and pay attention to your staff. They will tell you when they are becoming unsatisfied.

Never get so caught up in the day-to-day that you forget to hear what's going on around you.

Power Thought

A truly great boss or manager has a "the buck stops here" and a "broad shoulders" mentality.

Did you know that the interview process is a great marketing tool? People who are genuinely interested in your company will apply for positions, not just those looking for a job. It's possible to have an audience of up to 500 applicants who want to work for you. While you can't possibly hire them all, you do have a powerful opportunity to make a long-lasting impression.

If you respond to your applicants in a timely and courteous manner, they will remember. I have received hundreds of thank you notes for rejection letters. Because of the vulnerability of the candidates, you *will* make an impression, good or bad. They may never want to frequent your business again because they felt they were treated poorly. They will also never forget how great you were because you kept them in the loop.

Somehow, we have gotten away from responding to our potential employees as potential customers. We have decided that we don't have to respond to them, they don't deserve a response or we don't have the time or money to do it. The next wave of successful companies will be those who invite people to apply and who respond to them along every step. Be Bold. Be Different. And Respond!

Power Thought

Being courteous will separate you from everyone else.

A Rose Is Not Always as Sweet, No Matter What You Call It!

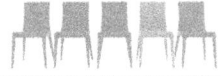

I was helping a local non-profit with their interview process, when an application for "Andre" came across my desk with decent qualifications. As I glanced over the cover letter, I noticed the candidate signed that letter as "Andrea." I was confused about what to call this person, so I didn't. As employers, we can be swayed by a person's technical skills, where they went to school, who they have worked for, but if they can't get their own name right ... no thank you.

Power Thought

Never forget that: Every. Detail. Matters.

I called a woman recently to schedule her for an interview. She thanked me for calling and let me know she would not be available because she would be getting a face lift that next week. On a separate occasion, I interviewed a woman who showed up to the interview completely disheveled and explained (unapologetically) that she had been gardening and simply forgot about the interview.

These two candidates have one major thing in common: neither prioritized the interview. When hiring, you want to look for people who are eager to interview! That passion will translate into passion for the job as well as for your company. When candidates are not committed to interviewing for you then that's exactly how they'll treat the job, should they be hired.

Power Thought

Hire the candidate who can dedicate time to interview
with you free of the distractions of facelifts and gardens.

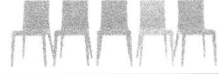

I have interviewed a great number of candidates who complain about younger generations having "no work ethic." Says who?! There are some young people who have no work ethic. There are also some Baby Boomers with no work ethic. Believe me, I have interviewed them. On the other hand, I've also interviewed and hired hardworking, A-list candidates anywhere from 17 to 85.

When discussing the topic of the baby boomers calling younger generations lazy, my 96-year-old grandmother laughed and said, "We used to say the same thing about them." To judge an entire population based on age is inaccurate and could cause you to overlook the perfect person to fill your job. Each generation always has something to say about the others and probably always will, but it's your job to keep that out of the interviews.

Power Thought

All stereo types have exceptions.
Your job is to search for those exceptions.

Sadly, I hear this comment more often than I care to. As an employer, why would I want to give you a job that you would hate? My clients and I want candidates that come to the table with enthusiasm and a positive attitude. If a criterion for the next position includes a "job that I won't hate" pass immediately. A positive outlook is a choice by the candidate and a must-have job requirement for any employer. I'm sure you'd want to hire someone looking for a job that they'll *love* not simply a job they won't hate.

Power Thought

Having a glass-full mentality is a choice anyone can make.

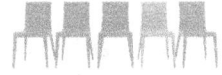

I recently interviewed 14 people with my clients. Exhausted, one of them looked over at me with wide eyes and said, "How do you *do* this all day?" Because I love it! I love the interview process, especially when I see each client's light bulbs go off about the process. They get it. They have made a great choice, and they know it. The candidate is also happy because the client is sure of their choice.

Soon after, I followed up with another client. I have helped this person hire many people for a variety of different positions. When asked how everyone was doing in their new positions, the response was, "All of our people are great. Thanks for your help!"

Why then is the interview process so hard? In my experience, the main reason is that the interview team is not prepared. A lot of work that must happen long before posting that job ad. Keep in mind:

- You can't get what you want, unless you know what you want.

- Your team has to be prepared, understanding who is responsible for the variety of tasks and roles necessary in the interview process.

- An interview is an interaction unlike any other in our culture. You can't just wing it and expect it to work.

I encourage you to put in the time upfront to examine what your ideal candidate looks like and to prepare your team. It will be well worth it in the end. When I follow up with you after your next interview process, you too can say, "Beth, our people are amazing!"

Power Thought

If you're prepared for whatever you want to do,
you can do whatever you've prepared for.

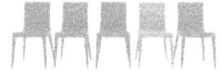

Listening is the cornerstone for conducting a successful interviewing process. I can't say this often enough! While listening to the candidate to measure integrity and skillset sounds obvious, it is also important for the interviewer to listen to *themselves*. The voice inside your head will sound the alarm bells if something is not quite right. If there is something worrying you that you can't articulate, ask for help. Schedule another interview and have someone sit in on it with you. Whatever you do, don't ignore it! Hiring someone is a big responsibility, so take the time to do it right by listening to your candidate *and* yourself.

Power Thought

Call it intuition, a hunch, or a gut feeling—Follow it!
Don't ignore it.

Your superstar employee is at home, pregnant. An amazing employee's father is dying of cancer. Your right hand-man injured himself in a Rugby game. For these employees, you will do whatever it takes to help them get back up and running. You will bend over backwards to accomplish whatever is needed to help them because you know the effort is appreciated and will be reciprocated. Then, you have that one employee who always spends their accrued vacation hours before they have really earned them. When they call in sick, you grit your teeth and seethe. Life happens, yet you are bothered. The question is: Why do some situations bother you with some employees and not with others?

The big difference is that your rock star employee will have a contingency plan in place so that work gets done despite life's interruptions. They will work from home when their child is sick, or they will make plans to cover their job, if they need to suddenly leave town. It isn't their job to do that, but they do it anyway as a way to contribute to the team and the core values of the company. That extra little something they do to make your life easier is why you will work hard to make them happy. Those who don't aren't really team members.

Power Thought

Superstar employees solve their own problems,
so that you don't have to.

Last week while I was interviewing a client, I kept smelling bacon. It smelled so good! I felt like that dog in the Beggin' Strips commercial whose sole focus was to get some bacon. I turned to my client and said, "I must be going crazy because I think I smell bacon!"

She laughed and replied "You aren't crazy. Our staff makes lunch together, and they usually cook breakfast foods." As I rounded the hallway to see for myself what was taking place, there were five people with plates piled high with bacon, eggs, pancakes and French toast crammed into one little office around an even smaller desk, sharing a meal together.

Company culture can be created in so many ways, and it doesn't have to cost a lot or take up much time. These staff members not only enjoyed their bacon, they were able to talk about work in a casual way. They created friendships and deeper relationships over those amazing pancakes while passing the syrup. Ask any of the employees and they will tell you that those brunches are fun *and* productive.

If your company is lagging behind, or employee morale is low, it might be time to introduce some fun.

I would love to hear from you if you or your employees introduced a morale boosting activity that has become part of your company culture?

Power Thought

Making bacon together can help you
bring home the bacon!

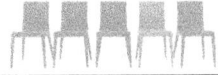

I was meeting with a new client to discuss the possibility of hiring their right-hand person. As I do with every client, I asked her to dream big. "If you could have any person you wanted for this job, who would they be and what would they know?"

Do you know what she said? "I want them to be punctual."

When you make a bad hire, tell yourself, "Well, I can work with this employee if only they do xyz." Then, xyz doesn't happen. Then you might say, "If only they will do abc, then I can work with that." Of course, abc isn't going to happen either. The next thing you know, you are wishing for someone to be punctual.

What if you changed the word "punctual" to "committed"? If someone is committed to the job and committed to the company, then they will be punctual.

I dare you to dream big around your next hiring decision. Think roses and rainbows, to infinity and beyond. Conduct effective interviews and you will find your dream employee!

Power Thought

Dreams are the substance of reality.

Do You Hire a "Payton Manning" or a "Tim Tebow"?

Both Peyton Manning and Tim Tebow are no longer in the NFL. However, each person represents a type of person you might want to hire. When making a good hiring decision, a boss must first ask, "Can I work with this person? Both Tebow and Manning had solid reputations for being workable, and in this era of cranky celebrities, this was a point for both of them.

The next question: Can they do the job? While Tebow was somewhat inconsistent, so was Peyton Manning. While Manning had experience on his side, he was also injured and set in his ways.

The third question: Is the candidate passionate about the job? Manning was a little crusty around the edges. He was also a leader in the lockout with the NFL. Tebow loved the game of football. He was energetic, passionate and needed coaching.

My vote? Hire a "Manning" to train a "Tebow." You will have experience coupled with passion and healthiness. That is a winning combination.

Power Thought

Pass the ball from the experienced to the inexperienced.
This is a game plan that ensures success.

With sweaty palms and a dry cotton mouth, Jane Smith opened the door and walked in. She approached the greeter and requested to meet with a certain person. She checked her hair and makeup in her hand mirror, then tried desperately to calm her nervous stomach. When she looked up, she saw the person that she was meeting, and she took a deep breath. *Here we go,* she thought. Is this a date or a job interview?

On the outside, the excitement of the first meeting, nerves and newness of it all, make the interaction of an interview comparable to a first date. Candidates are in a vulnerable state when they walk into a job interview and going on a first date can produce similar feelings of vulnerability. But are they the same?

The biggest difference between a date and a job interview is the power of the interviewer over the candidate. The interviewer decides when the interview will take place, its location, time of day, the agenda, whether there will be a second interview, whether the candidate gets the position or whether the candidate receives a "no thank you" for the position. All of the power sits with the employer. In dating, the two people come to the table as equals.

This power difference is why employers struggle with interviewing. They are often as uncomfortable with the power differentiation as the candidate; they are unsure of how to get around an environment that brings about one individual's desire to please and the other's role to choose. Their sole desire is to make a good assessment for their next hire, yet candidates are just telling them what they want to hear. And of course they are! They are trying to find a job and willing to bear sweaty palms!

Bottom line: dating and hiring are not the same.

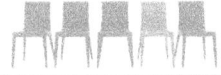

Power Thought

You are the boss, not the date. Don't forget that.

When my 11-year-old daughter Katy flew on an airplane by herself for the very first time, I was a nervous wreck! I had a hard time focusing on work; I kept checking my phone to see if I had messages saying she had landed safely. Katy, of course, was fine. In fact, she had a great time during her first solo flight and learned a valuable lesson in independence. I realized the more she can do for herself, the better equipped she will be in the future when dealing with unexpected situations.

You may ask what any of this has to do with interviewing. As I impatiently waited for the phone to ring, I realized that I need to provide my clients with the same level of independence. While I certainly adore helping each of my clients interview their next great employee, I also realize that I need to get them better prepared to do interviewing by themselves. Again, the more prepared they are in their businesses, the easier it is to handle unexpected personnel issues.

In the past, my typical process was to create and submit job ads, help develop job descriptions, vet interview candidates, schedule interview times, and then perform the actual interviews in front of my client. We would then do a "dash board" review in between interviews to uncover what we learned from each candidate, based on speech patterns, phrasing, and responses to my A-list candidate questions. Rarely, did I actually hand the interview process over to my client. They have certainly learned from the experience; 91 percent of the time they retained the ideal employee they were seeking. But I realized that my mission with A-list Interviews is to transform the world through the interview process to create happy, healthy work environments for all. This cannot be achieved until I give my clients the gift of independence by empowering them to run effective interviews long after I am gone.

From now on, I will be including a hand-over process, and I will be teaching my clients how to interview by themselves through the program I have developed called "A-list Interviews 7 Steps to Finding Amazing Employees." This program has worked successfully in all walks of business; I am excited to help my clients develop their own comfort levels around the interview process. When they fly solo, I will still be a nervous wreck because I really want my clients to succeed, but I will know that I set them up for success. The world will be transformed through the interview process by hundreds of interviewers, not just me. And there is no better feeling than that!

Power Thought

Letting go is often the hardest thing you'll ever do.

© Randy Glasbergen. www.glasbergen.com

GLASBERGEN

"I don't know what sort of salary you're offering,
but on my last job I made a lot of dough!"

While rocking my infant daughter years ago, I began instinctively doing what adults have done for centuries; I began singing lullabies to her "When the wind blows the cradle will rock,

When the bough breaks, the cradle will fall, And down will come baby ... ."

Then I stopped. I suddenly listened to the words that I was about to sing! I said aloud, "What kind of fool puts an infant in a cradle at the top of a tree and watches them fall?!" Horrified, I changed the words: "... right into Mama's arms." Ahhh, much better. My daughter was raised singing Rock-A-Bye Baby with a much better ending. To this day, I am not sure that she even knows the original words to that song, which suits me just fine.

In the interview process, I teach people that the best skill to have is listening for word choice. I train them to stop and really *listen* to the words used by the candidate, and digest their meanings as they relate to the position for which we are hiring. When you listen to the word choices of your candidate, they will tell you what you need to hear in order to make a great hiring decision. Word choices will expose blamers, know-it-alls, pass the buckers, and more. When the interview is over, if you feel the candidate did not give you enough information, review your notes. The words you need to listen for are in there.

As an interviewer, your primary job is to pay attention to the word choices used by your potential employees. And be careful to not just hear what you want to hear; it means the difference between a decent employee and an A-list player. If any "boughs break" in your business, who would you rather have waiting at the bottom of the tree?

Power Thought

An astute person hears what is really being said,
not what they want to hear.

Most people who watch the Olympics experience some surprises regarding performances from our athletes. However, if we actually listened to the athletes talk about their goals, we may have fewer surprises:

- Danell Leyva: "I want to win a medal." So he did, a bronze

- John Orazco: "I just want to go to the Olympics." So he did. He was a top-10 finisher.

- Gabby Douglas: "I want to make history." So she did. She is the first African American woman to win a gold medal in Gymnastics. She won two.

When interviewing candidates, you can predict the success of your new hire by listening to their language around their goals in an interview. Writing down exactly what your candidate has to say can prevent performance surprises later down the road and lead your team to gold rated success!

Power Thought
Whether sports or business,
the bottom line is performance.

When a client calls me to help them screen and interview candidates, they are usually in a hurry. They need me to get started *today*, and frankly, they really needed me to start three weeks ago. The "hurry up" syndrome is a common issue at A-list Interviews. However, hurrying through the interview process never works. Making a bad hiring decision just to put a "butt in the seat" is always more costly than having a little patience and truly screen and interview until you find your ideal new employee. In his book *Preventing Internal Theft* author Robert Plotkin, who says, "It is better to operate short-handed for a period of time and rely on your existing staff to cover ... than hiring someone unqualified or inappropriate for the establishment." I could not agree more.

As painful as it may seem to wait for the right person to come along in your interview process, it is always way more painful to bring a person onboard who is the wrong fit for your company. Consider the other factors that are included in hiring a misfit for your organization: reduce efficiency and downtime for training, morale within the organization, the customer experience of a person who is not in alignment with the company, just to name just a few. In the end, when you bring in a new employee just to fill a position, the likelihood that you will end up back in the interview process within the six months is incredibly high. Stick to our A-list motto of "find the right employee the first time" and you will save yourself more time, money and headaches than you can imagine. The right employee is always worth the wait.

Power Thought

Good employees come to those who wait. Be patient.
Your Rock Star employee is one their way!

Are You Becoming the Micro-Manager You Never Wanted to Be?

I recently overheard a man complaining to his business partner about his administrative assistant.

"She just does not do the things that she is supposed to do! And then, I find her leaving early. I swear that I have told her 100 times to put our marketing packets together, and they are still not finished," he said, frustrated. "What do I do?"

His business partner replied, "Well, we need to set up a plan for her. We need to say to her that she needs to complete three packets a day every day next week."

"While I am writing this plan for her, I might as well write down everything that she is *not* doing," he sighed. "I have never thought of myself as a micro manager."

For the next hour, these two gentlemen wrote down a schedule for the administrator. It included a lunch break and goals for exactly what they wanted her to do ... basically a plan for how he would continue to micro manage her.

Why do we become micro managers? Rarely do I meet managers who *love* to micro manage; in fact, most of them hate it. However, they do find it necessary at times to keep people on track. If you find yourself micro managing your employees, examine why this change has occurred. Here are a few reasons:

- *The job changed.* It could be that the job responsibilities have changed, and no one has communicated this to the employee. If that is the case, get out your job description and review it with your employee. Begin the conversation with, "I have noticed that we have some duties that are falling through the cracks. Do you have thoughts about that?" Give them the opportunity to give input.

- *Your job changed.* Managers sometimes fail to realize that if their job has changed, the admin's responsibilities may have changed too and usually with no warning. Your admin may be frustrated that they are expected to do something that they do not know how to do. You need to make sure they have the training and skills to be successful in the position.

- *Your admin changed.* Sometimes people need to move on to another position, and it is your job as their manager to help them leave gracefully. You might begin the conversation with, "It seems that you are not happy in your current role. Can you tell me about that?"

- *You hired the wrong person.* Last but not least, you might not have the right person in that role. If your admin does not love their job, you can either find another job for them or find another admin.

No matter the case, your job is to have a conversation with the employee and create an environment of accountability, not micro management. Make sure the tasks and duties are agreed upon and written down. Realize that micro management is a short-term solution to a long-term problem. Use it wisely and sparingly.

Power Thought

Constantly looking over someone's shoulder
will make you both unhappy.

I have read multiple articles about writing resumes, and the primary school of thought is that a candidate has three seconds to capture the attention of the hiring manager. The resume has to be easy to scan, because the hiring manager is looking at hundreds of resumes, and they will only look at the candidate for three seconds. Did you know that the same is true for candidates looking at job ads?

When a candidate is applying for jobs online, they will review many job ads in one sitting, and apply to those jobs that sound appealing. How do you write a job ad that stands out? Here are a few tips:

- *Do not use your job description as your job ad.* Usually job descriptions are long and tedious to read, so candidates will not spend the time to read them fully and completely. They will scan the description, and you have three seconds to capture their interest.

- *Use your mission statement in the first line of the ad.* Candidates want to know their work is playing a part in something larger than themselves. They want to know their work matters, so tell them *why* your company is doing what it does.

- *Keep it short.* Begin with your mission statement, use a few bullet points to tell candidates what you are looking for, and then give clear instructions on how to apply. You can always give candidates more information as the interview process continues.

When you are writing your job ad, remember this is a marketing piece. Make the ad a direct reflection of the job, the mission and the values of your company. It is an invitation for candidates to apply, and you want the tone to be positive. At the end of the day, you only have three seconds ... .

Power Thought

Being clear and concise in all you do will benefit everyone.

When my daughter Katy was eight, we were having a girls' night in, complete with the Texas Longhorn football game, pajamas and of course, pizza. I asked her if she wanted to go with me to go pick up our food, and she enthusiastically agreed. Appearing to be ready, she had on her pajama shorts, fuzzy purple slippers and her fleece peace sign jacket.

I said, "It's 49 degrees outside. You might want to change your pants."

When she came out of her room with her chocolate brown moose pj bottoms, she looked at me, looked down at her pants, and giggling said, "This does not match! Now I have to change my shirt!"

After that, she had to change her jacket, until finally we left to get dinner. We laughed hysterically about the change of clothes from the bottoms up!

Many of my clients look at hiring exactly the same way as my daughter got dressed. They react to the circumstances as opposed to having a plan. When the pants leave, we will make the new pants work with the old shirt, even though the materials are all wrong and the outfit doesn't suit the occasion. With just a bit of planning, changing your pants doesn't have to ruin your whole outfit. How do you plan to avoid wardrobe mismatches? Here are three tips:

- *Take the time to look at your entire outfit.* Before hiring anyone, you must be certain of who you need and why you need them. Look at the vision for your company. Where are you going? What type of skills and people will get you there? Think big. Then define your ideal candidate on paper.

- *Write the job description.* Re-write the past version if you have one; do not just reuse the old one. What worked before may not work now. Look at the position from a new perspective and re-create it; you have a golden opportunity to transform this role.

- *Pull it all together when writing your ad.* This is where you put the finishing touches on the position. Invite people to apply by sharing your vision, the ideal person description and technical skills required. Make it appealing to attract the person you are seeking.

To capture the attention of candidates, your presentation of your company is key. Be prepared. Make sure the ideal candidate list matches the job description, which in turn matches the ad. It's the entire outfit that makes the difference, not only to the candidate, but also ensures that you hire the right fit. Don't just change your pants—create a whole new look!

Power Thought

How you present yourself will determine
how others receive you.

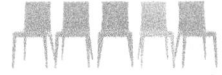

I am fostering puppies! Well, really my daughter is fostering puppies, and I am along for the ride. The back story is that "PawsCo" brings puppies who are in high-kill shelters in locations all across Colorado up to the Denver metro area. They vaccinate the dogs, get them cleaned up and host adoption events at PetSmart and other locations to help find forever homes for these awesome animals. Our role is to foster the puppy for a few days until the forever home is found.

We were volunteering at an adoption event, and I noticed that every person who walked by had a story to tell about a current family dog, or about a dog that they had as a child and how much joy this animal brought to their lives. The stories they told were beautiful and inspiring. The best part is watching an unhappy, tired, grumpy person become transformed by the love and joy remembered when they describe their beloved companion.

I have to ask the question, what would it be like if you felt this way about your employee? In my training classes and in searches we conduct for clients who are hiring, we always start by dreaming about the best employee they have ever had. We then focus on how we can emulate finding an employee that brings satisfaction. Watching my clients transform from frustrated employers with open positions to fill into a smiling, relaxed client who just hired their next incredible employee is just like watching these adorable puppies go to their forever homes—utterly priceless, and I love it! This is what life is all about.

If you are thinking about a puppy, an older dog, or a cat, go to www.pawsco. org and pick one out. If you are looking to hire an incredible employee, call me. I can help.

Power Thought

Hire the *best!* Nothing else will do.

I was conducting some phone interviews with a client. On a particular call, the interview was going well until the candidate surprised me with a request: "Can I put you on hold and take this other call?"

"Uh, sure," I mumbled. While I waited, listening to really bad background music, I contemplated this question: Does this candidate really want *this* job?" The resounding answer came to me: No, he really does not. If he really wanted the job that my client was offering, he would have ignored any and all calls, no matter who was calling him. At this point, nothing else mattered; his skills, his experience, his ability to do the job, none of those counted, because if he did not *want* the job, he is not going to *do* the job.

The last thing that you want to do is hire someone who is not willing to talk to you long enough to find out if this is the job for them, or hire someone who is not absolutely thrilled to come and work for you. Put this job offer on hold, just like the candidate did to me, and wait for the right candidate to come along. They will come to you if you are patient. You will be so glad that you waited!

Power Thought

Be courteous and respectful.
Turn off your phone in interviews.

I interviewed a woman via Skype with one of my out-of-state clients. When my video popped up, she said, "Wow, you look like Godzilla!"

For the past three weeks, I have been racking my brain trying to figure out how being compared to a slobbery, atomic mutant reptile can possibly be a compliment ... maybe I am bigger than life? Loud? Dry skin? The more important concept to consider here is how an outburst like this might affect your clients. If she said this to an important client of yours or a big donor, they might be unwilling to sign that contract you have been waiting for. They might not want to do business with you. People have pulled their business for a lot less than being called Godzilla. Meanwhile, we will be looking for another candidate and I will be moisturizing heavily ☺.

Power Thought

Choose your words carefully because
you can never get them back.

After an interview with a great candidate, my clients usually want to hire that person on the spot. They feel strongly they have waited long enough, and they want to get this person on board ASAP.

While I completely understand their desires, I ask them to think about the interview for at least 24-48 hours. The reason for the waiting period is that your thoughts are often different outside of the interview, especially if you give your thoughts a chance to simmer. Think about it like you think about soup in a crock pot. Similar to making a soup where you initially collect and prep all of your ingredients, a company preps by putting together an ideal list for the best candidate, writing a job description, writing a job ad, and posting the job. The job then simmers on the job boards as applicants begin to submit resumes, compared to the soup simmering in the crockpot. The employers then get the resumes and begin interviewing, like adding spices to the soup and continuing to let it simmer. Throw in some vision and dreaming, your crock pot will make some pretty great tasting soup! Eat the soup too early and the spices may have not soaked in yet. If you wait too long, the vegetables turn to mush, and the soup is not as good.

Give yourself the extra time to absorb the experience, just like the soup absorbs the spices. Your experience will be way better for the wait.

Power Thought

Emotions, good and bad, can cloud objective judgment.

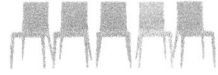

When Katy was a little girl, she loved to play with Mr. and Mrs. Potato Head. Some of her creations were hilarious: an arm being in the ear hole, lips in the eye hole, or Mrs. Potato Head walking around on a hat instead of shoes. Part of the brilliance of that game is taking all of the parts and making a whole, no matter how it looks to someone else. Once, Katy dressed up Mrs. Potato Head with shoes, lips, two arms, two eyes, and ... a mustache on her head. She looked up at me with those big blue eyes and said, "Mommy, doesn't Mrs. Potato Head look beautiful?

I had a client who was getting really frustrated with the search we were conducting. He looked at me and said, "If I could just take attributes from one candidate and put it with the skillset from the other candidate, I would be hiring someone today!"

You might identify with my client's frustration but this is good news. When you start to see what you *want* from an employee, even though it is in two people, your ideal candidate is right around the corner. All you need to do is piece together what is important to you, and that person will show up. It is indeed a beautiful thing!

Power Thought

Putting together your vision, and seeing it come to reality,
is a beautiful experience.

I am fairly certain that none of you know my full name is Margaret Elizabeth Smith. When I was about five months old, my parents called me "the baby" until Mom got pregnant with my brother. My folks figured out that calling me "the baby" was short-lived, for obvious reasons, and they had better come up with something to call me. Mom tried, "Maggie, Margaret and Meg."

Dad didn't like any of those so he tried, "Liza, Liz and Lizzie."

Mom replied, "Over my dead body."

Then Dad came home with Beth, and it stuck … sort of. Dad calls me "Bethy-Boo," Mom calls me "Bethie," my friend calls me "B," my nieces and nephews call me "Aunt B" and my beloved grandfather called me "Becky."

Last year, my daughter Katy entered the 6th grade at the ripe old age of 12 and she decided that calling me "Mom" was for babies, so she began calling me "Bethly." Her friends even now call me "Befly." I must be a total whack job, because I answer to any of these!

I have seen so many ads with crazy job titles on them. For example, there was an ad for an admin position "Chief Administrative Officer" and my immediate reaction was, "Here is a C-level position that I have never heard of before!" Until I read the complete job ad that included answering the phones and opening the mail, I was under the impression this job position was higher than entry level. It was confusing. If I am confused—and I read job ads all the time—imagine what the candidates must experience. Call the job what it is, so that people recognize themselves in the job they are applying for. Just because I am crazy and answer to 10 different derivatives of my name, doesn't mean your candidates will. Happy Name Calling!

Power Thought

Titles can be smoke and mirrors,
or can represent true authority.

When my daughter moved to college, I took two weeks off to help her. While this brought about a mix of emotions, I knew how important it was for me to be with Katy as she started her college journey.

This brings up an important topic that I preach to my clients often: Everyone needs time away from work, whether it be for important milestones in their personal lives, or for a vacation that allows them time to rejuvenate, recuperate, and come back to work in a better mindset!

The fact is that people need time away from work, even when you own the company, like me. Some of my clients get really excited when a candidate tells them in an interview that they *never* take vacations. I think this is terrible! Inspiration rarely comes to someone sitting in their office, answering emails. Inspiration comes from experience, and when the conscious mind is not consumed with a particular topic, and usually happens outside of the office.

As a nation, we are not good at taking vacation. We feel that we can't get away and we can't unplug because we might miss something. I think we miss things when we *don't* take time off.

When your employees want to take vacation time, praise him or her for doing so. Say thank you. Then ask the employee what you can do to help facilitate his or her vacation time so they are not performing work while away. Not only will they think that you are the greatest boss ever, but they will come back recharged, renewed and inspired. Your business will benefit and, therefore, so will you. Maybe then you can take some time off, too!

I was back in the saddle soon enough, grateful I took the time to be with Katy, and was ready to tackle work with renewed energy and vision. As a bonus for my time with her, I also had a killer tan!

Power Thought

There is a time to work and a time to rest,
and productivity comes from doing both.

Sand on the stage, beach balls in the air and Parrot heads! This was the scene at the Pepsi Center several years ago for a Jimmy Buffett concert I attended. The back-up singers and dancers began rousing the crowd to get into the groove, which reached a feverish frenzy until finally, the man himself stepped out onto the stage to a packed house of screaming fans. If you have never been to a Jimmy Buffett concert, it is hard to describe how the music started, the colors of the lights flashing and just how enamored I was with the entire scene, especially because right before the concert, I was the lucky holder of a backstage pass to meet a legend himself!

Meeting Mr. Buffett was indeed a lifetime experience, and one that I keep living over and over. I relay the story often to my friends, colleagues and now you. However, because you were not there, you probably do not have the same attachment to the story as I do. Shaking his hand, listening to the crowd in the background, and having my photo taken with him was truly amazing. But since you were not there, it is not possible for you to have the same relationship with Jimmy that I now have. After all, listening to Margaritaville on your iPod is just not the same.

Now you may be asking how this relates to interviewing for employees. Imagine that you send your very capable team to an interview with a candidate. Then imagine your team trying to describe the interaction to you in a manner that encompasses all facets of the interview. It is not the same thing as meeting with the candidate face to face. Even when your team takes great notes and really listens to the candidate, they will not be able to fully describe the interview in its entirety. No one can, anymore that you could possibly grasp the unique experience of meeting Jimmy Buffett. In order to fully experience a candidate's interview, you have to be in the room with them. You have to shake their hand and see how they interact with you in order to know if this candidate will be a good fit for your open position. With approximately two-thirds of all hires being mistakes, and the money those mistakes cost, can you really afford to short change an interview process by not being present?

Power Thought
First-hand knowledge beats second-hand information
every time.

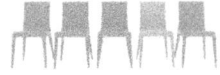

To stay fit, I have been swimming six days a week: five days a week with a Master's group and a private lesson on day six. A few weeks ago, my coach asked me to swim a "fail-set"—15 laps in a certain time frame that get harder and harder as you go. The purpose is that you will fail. You can't help it. This is why it is called a fail-set, but failing isn't really the point. What is important is *when* you fail and what you do as a result.

The same process of failing can happen in interviewing. You will post your job ad, interview many people who you will not want to hire and will need to start the entire process over. You will go through a lot of candidates and find that you have to re-post your job ad and begin the process over again. You will get tired, frustrated and want to quit. As your interviewing coach, my job is to encourage you to keep going and to keep your eye on the final prize of hiring the best person for the position and your company. When you have the right person on your team, your life will be so much easier, the company will grow and your clients will be satisfied!

Are you wondering about my fail-set? I failed on lap #11 out of 15. I sat one out, re-grouped, and finished my last three laps. My coach was very pleased, and I walked away satisfied, knowing that I got through my fail-set ... swimmingly.

Power Thought

The saying, "If at first you don't succeed, try, try again" is always in vogue.

While visiting my clients to get input for this book about the interview process, I heard some awesome success stories, like the one from my client, Steve. We hired his right-hand employee a little over two years ago. Steve tells me that he now has the drama-free office environment that he has always wanted. As a matter of fact, he now takes Fridays off and is making more money! To give you an example of just how great it is to be Steve, he faces a bi-annual audit as he is in the financial industry. The audit process has typically taken about four hours with the auditor and several weeks of Steve's time to prepare. This last audit took 45 minutes and Steve's right-hand person prepared the entire document!

Lesson learned: Great hires = more time and more money. Are you ready to get started on your A-list hire?

Power Thought

When you hire people who love their work,
you show just how smart you truly are.

I just read yet another article talking about how hiring with your gut never works. As a matter of fact, hiring on your gut reaction not only sets your employee up to fail, you will hold on to them longer, even though you know they are not right for the position, because your gut is involved. So, what exactly does all of this mean?

If you have been around me long enough, you have heard me say that your gut does not help you in the interview process, because the candidate is trying to sell to you. They want a job. They are anxious, worried, nervous and scared. They *will* tell you what you want to hear, because they want a job. Remember, an interview is not a normal interaction, so the normal dynamics are off. Therefore, your gut reaction will be skewed and will not help in making a good hiring decision.

Instead, I want you to go with your "but." The "but" is the potential big problem, the proverbial "pebble-in-your-shoe." You will talk about your potential employee like this: "I like this and this about her, *but*... she doesn't seem to want the job." "I really like XYZ about him, *but* he complained about the commute. If the 'but" is something that you can live with and will not bug you later on, then you can dismiss it from your hiring criteria. However, if you ignore it, you *will* make a bad hiring decision.

Go with your "but," not your gut. You can do it!

Power Thought

Ignoring your "but" will become a pain in your butt.

I've told you about my swimming experience, however, I recently had a setback. One day, I began to experience hip pain. The diagnosis was a herniated disc in my back. Much to my dismay, I have had to quit swimming and go into rehabilitation mode to regain my health. I was at a crossroads and needed to make a decision about my swim lessons. I really did not want to quit working with my coach but swimming was no longer an option. After some deliberation, I decided to meet him for coffee one morning to give him the bad news. He immediately suggested that a treatment option could be trigger point massage work, and lo and behold, he is a certified Myotherapist. He was right! The trigger point along with chiropractic did the trick. Our business relationship has changed direction from when we started working together, and I could never have predicted this amazing outcome.

As a business grows, the positions that you have within the company will also grow and change. The right hire will grow and change with you and your business. If you can remain flexible, you might be surprised at what other skills your great employee can bring to the table. The lesson is that no one can predict the future. We do not know how our businesses will change, but when you hire the right person, you can travel that journey together.

Power Thought

Flexibility is needed in business ... always!

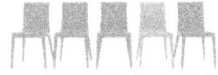

Every client that I work with wants a certain level of experience for the position they want filled. They say, "Beth, the person needs to have five years of experience. Not negotiable."

The problem with experience is that it is a mixed bag. According to the book *Talent is Overrated*, "... people with lots of experience were no better at their jobs than those with very little experience." Are you shocked? The book goes on to say, "Researchers from the INSEAD business school in France and the US Naval Postgraduate School call the phenomenon 'the experience trap.'" Their key finding is that while companies typically value experienced managers, rigorous study shows that, on average "managers with experience did not produce high caliber results."

If experience does not make for a good hire, what does? Basically, you are looking for three traits in good hires:

- *Can they handle conflict resolution?* Whether there is conflict with the boss or conflict with a team member, how does this person resolve it? Basically, if your employee needs *you* to solve *their* problems for them, then that is what you will spend your time doing. It is called management.

- *Can they do the job?* This sounds like experience, right? It is not. It is more about basic communication and teamwork. Do they want to help the customer? Do they take ownership of their work? Do they ask for help when they need it? These are the qualities of an employee who is self-sufficient and motivated to get the job done.

- *Do they want the job?* Are they passionate about the work they do? If so, then they do not mind the occasional drudgery of the job. They love to solve the problems of the position and are motivated to innovate.

If you want to hire good people, do not get caught in the experience trap. Find the person who can solve conflict, has basic customer service skills and the passion for the job, then train, train, train. In the end you will have to manage less. You will be so glad that you did!

Power Thought

Conflict will always drive true character and
motives to the surface.

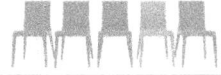

The end of the year is always a time of reflection for me. I like to look back and see the difference I have made in the lives of others and plan for how I will continue to bring value in the coming year.

I had started to plan the publication of my first book "Why Can't I hire Good People?" back in 2014. During the process of publishing, I was given the unique opportunity to interview my clients to learn more about how I have assisted them with better hiring practices. Below is one such testimonial I received that brought tears of joy to my eyes. I hope you enjoy reading it as much as I... .

One of my clients hired me two years ago to find an Executive Director. "Our Board had a very poor hiring record," said the Board President at the time of the hire. "We floundered for a number of years. We would hire folks because they were local, and we'd sit down with them for a chat. This is not the best way to do business. The whole experience with A-list Interviews was so different for us, in that we sat back and observed, and let the expert keep us on track. We made decisions very quickly. We now have a successful operation that runs seamlessly, and we are reaching goals that we never dreamed possible."

Our newly hired Executive Director, said, "How has A-list changed our organization? I now have a cohesive team of people, and our budget has increased by $300,000 in the two years since I got here. Our attendance has doubled, our events have doubled. I now understand the importance of looking past experience and skills—I need to find the right fit and develop them. It has worked out fabulously!"

It was a great way to end 2013! I continue to reflect back at the end of each year and reflect forward to each New Year ... and I encourage you to do the same.

Power Thought
Reflecting back allows you to consider
the possibilities going forward.

I love it when an opportunity presents itself to listen in on a "normal" interview. Arriving early for an appointment at a Starbucks in the Denver area, I was enjoying an amazing cup of black tea as the store manager began interviewing for a potential staff member. As effective interviewing is my passion, I was fascinated by the exchange I observed.

First, the candidate entered the Starbucks as I did at 12:45. She sat nervously waiting for 15 minutes to begin the interview for her next potential position. While the manager did begin the interview at exactly 1:00 (kudos to her) a huge opportunity to set up the candidate for immediate success was missed. An A-list candidate will *always* be 15 minutes early for an interview, especially for a position they are really interested in. If the interviewer actually leaves them waiting for 15 minutes, the candidate becomes more nervous, thus increasing the chances of blowing the interview.

Second, the manager talked for the entire interview, occasionally glancing at the resume of the candidate. The candidate very dutifully nodded her head (She will need a massage after this!) and laughed at all the manager's jokes. In a truly effective interview, the hiring manager should be engaging in active listening, rather than explaining the position and requirements. If the manager is talking rather than asking questions, the candidate does not have the chance to share skills, abilities, and personality with the manager. By not listening, the manager really has very little knowledge about the applicant or how they can truly contribute to the team.

Third, the manager got up and left the table twice to handle other issues and the candidate was left sitting by herself. Now I realize life can be full of interruptions. However, during an interview, the only focus should be around the task at hand: assessing the skill set and cultural fit of the potential new employee. Continuous interruptions reduce the hiring manager's ability to determine fit and the candidate's confidence about the job environment.

Fourth, the manager interviewed this woman in front of an audience of roughly ten people waiting for their coffee drinks. The interview lasted 42 minutes. For 42 minutes this candidate was not only vulnerable and exposed to a hiring manager, but to an entire audience of people. Don't hold interviews in public, high traffic areas. Respect is a cornerstone for any great relationship and public interviews are very disrespectful.

Last, but certainly not least, the manager discussed the highpoints of the candidate with another worker behind the counter, again in front of an audience. Do I really need to point out how disrespectful this is?

After my observances, I realized this is a perfect example of a "normal" interview, meaning that most people conduct interviews just like this and wonder why they can't hire good people. I honestly do not believe this hiring manager was even aware of her interviewing style and its ineffectiveness towards hiring a great employee. My big question is this: Was this manager really ever taught how to conduct an interview? Did she feel supported through the process, so that she could be successful in her hiring decisions? Did she really have the tools and environment needed to be successful in her decision-making process?

Employers who truly desire amazing staff need to support their hiring managers by teaching them how to interview. Give them the proper tools to find the next generation of A-list employees needed to grow the business. This is the gift that keeps on giving.

Power Thought

Give of yourself and you can be the gift that
keeps on giving.

I met with a new client who suffers from what I call the "Hiring Hangover." He had just fired a longtime employee and had to hire someone else quickly. The whole experience left a really bad taste in his mouth and he was having a hard time getting over it. He kept trying to change his policies and procedures to make sure that he did not get into the same position with a new employee that he had experienced in the past. In other words, he wanted to punish the new employee for the sins of the old employee. While this is completely understandable, it will not get you to where you want to go. When you hire a person while "hungover," you will make a bad hiring decision. You have to feel good about bringing a new person onboard. You have to be excited.

How do you recover from a bad hire? You take a deep breath. Do not hire too quickly. If you need immediate help, hire a temp. Jumping into a situation with a new hire when you are not ready sets you both up for failure. Create your ideal candidate list. Put your head in the clouds and dream *big*. And I mean really big, like roses and rainbows and unicorns. You cannot have what you want unless you know what it is and how to identify it. Until you are ready to write a list of what you want, then you are not ready for a new hire. Be patient. Do not start the interview process until you feel excited again.

Every manager has had a bad hire. It feels awful and firing someone should never feel good. Give yourself time to recover and breathe. Things will look better tomorrow. And your next amazing employee is right around the corner ... I promise.

Power Thought

In plain vernacular the word "grace" means, "That's okay, you're forgiven." Remember to extend grace to yourself.

One Friday I came home to a fish in a plastic cup on my kitchen counter. My daughter named him Harley. She promptly went out and bought him a really nice bowl with beautiful blue rocks, then filled the bowl with fresh water. When we put Harley in the fishbowl, I thought the fish was dead ... really. He laid on the bottom for a while, then he floated to the top. I tried to tell her that Harley was not going to make it, that he was dead in the water. She did not believe me and kept at it. She kept watching this fish, trying to keep it living through pure will. We watched it for hours before he finally began to swim around and attack the way-too-many-food pellets that we dropped in his new home. Two days later he was thriving; he looked like he was a brand-new fish with a new lease on life.

A client called last week frustrated with his employee of almost three years. Things were not getting done, balls were dropping and clients were not happy. I coached my client to sit down with his beloved employee and explain how he was feeling. Turns out, this really great employee needed fresh water and some attention. Remember, our employees are not us. They do not learn the job through osmosis; they learn it from their immediate supervisor. And they continue to perform and perfect as a result of that leadership.

If you are feeling like your staff is half-floating through their work, it is time for some attention. Show them that you are committed to their success by asking them how they are feeling about their work. Ask what you can do to help them enjoy their job better. And you know what? It might be shocking how easy it is to keep your employees engaged and happy with a committed boss who cares enough to ask, "Do you need some fresh water?"

As for Harley, it turns out that he was the subject of a science experiment in my daughter's science class. She "fish-napped" him because she said he looked dead.

I said, "Won't your teacher be mad that you stole the fish from the experiment?"

"Mom," she said with an eye roll. "The class is called 'Life Science,' emphasis on life!"

Well said, kiddo.

Power Thought

We all need reviving at times, and asking heartfelt
questions is a great way to revive others.

"You can name your own salary. I call mine Tiny Tim."

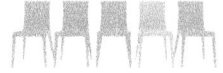

I went to parent/teacher conferences and met with Katy's science teacher. He began by asking if we had any questions that we specifically wanted to address, and I asked him if he was aware that Katy had stolen the fish from the science experiment. He laughed and said no. He thought that the fish had died and that someone had just thrown him away. I told him the story of Harley and how Katy had nursed him back to life, and I asked him if she was going to fail her experiment.

He said, "Absolutely not! The goal is to learn how to collect data every day in a scientific experiment that the kids set up themselves." Then, he smirked and added, "That story is awesome!"

I am asked all the time by my clients about how to encourage their employees to be more creative and innovative. That happens by letting your employees try new ways of doing things, even if the outcome isn't what you wanted. Mr. Leary is a wonderful example of a teacher who allows innovation and creativity in his classroom. He is flexible enough to let outcomes unfold without micro managing the process. In fact, he is thrilled to encourage passionate displays. Katy's science teacher is the epitome of a great leader, and we can all learn this from him: Innovation comes from trying new things, and sometimes, that means failing. We learn from both trying *and* failing. In addition, Katy learned to stand up for something she believes in with the support of the adults around her. You can't ask for a greater experience than that.

Thanks, Mr. Leary!

P.S. Harley thanks you, too!

Power Thought

While financial profit is the goal, there are many ways to
profit that will make your company richer in the long run.

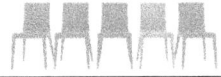

Last week, I placed a great employee in the right job with a great company, and everyone was excited. We all remember those moments in the interview process when we wanted to pull our hair out. You have candidates that just don't show up. You have the candidate that looks right at you and says, "Wow, I don't like doing that type of work" (True story). You have the potential employee who shows up late with no apology or excuse, then proceeds to interrupt you for the entire interview. Ugh! I have had days where I just wanted to bang my head against the interview table over and over... and over again.

Then, when you least expect it—when you think that you will *never* find the right person *ever*—your dream candidate walks through the door. They are on time, bring extra copies of resumes, references, and homework. They've done their research. They ask great questions and bring solutions, then they end the interview by telling you that this is their dream job. They make it through the entire process and they love the offer. And the kicker? They can start on Monday!

Every time I begin an interview process, I know that I am in for a roller coaster ride. I am going to laugh, cry, pull my hair out, bang my head on the table. Then I am going to laugh, because I'm so happy for my clients and the candidate they have found. I feel proud, because we got through the process and it is the right fit for all. Then I am going to shed a little tear, because the job is over. It is time for me to leave and go work with others, and the process starts all over again...with a sniff and a chuckle.

Power Thought

Every roller coaster has its "ups" and "downs."
It might even seem frightening at times,
but when it's over you're glad you took the ride.

Rejection is commonplace for business owners. We are often told that people are not interested in our products and services. Typically, we shrug it off and begin the pursuit of someone else who may really need our offerings. Yet, when we are in a position to offer a new employment opportunity, we are shocked when we receive a no thank you from a candidate.

For example, I was so excited for one of my clients when we extended an offer to a candidate. I was equally excited for another client when we invited a different candidate back for a third interview! However, both candidates declined, which tossed both of my clients into a bit of depression. Imagine how disheartening it was for them both to be so excited about a potential new hire, only to have the candidate demonstrate that they are not excited about the position.

Many of my business clients are stressed out, overworked, tired and sometimes completely panicked as they are hiring for a new or vacant position. My best advice is that "Rejection is Protection" and actually something to be very excited about. If someone does not want to work for you and they tell you that *before* you have hired them, you win! You are protected from poor quality work, absenteeism, and unsatisfied clients, because when someone *loves* their job, they perform. They give it their all, and both of you are happy. When you feel like you have been punched in the gut after a candidate rejects your position, learn to be grateful. Turn that negative into a positive. Turn lemons into lemonade and get ready to serve that lemonade to your new A-list candidate who is walking your way right this minute.

Power Thought

Rejection doesn't mean "no";
it means you are one step closer to "yes."

I always find the hiring process fascinating, especially when I begin working with people who have had employees on staff for an extended period of time who are not a good fit. They almost always say to me, "I knew it was not going to work out" after we get to a place where we are going to let go of an employee and begin searching for the perfect candidate to hire.

As many of my conversations go, I met with a potential new client who began the conversation with, "You have to know that I am *bad* at hiring."

I asked, "How do you know?"

The client replied, "Because I just fired the worst hire ever."

"When did you know that this employee was the worst hire ever?"

"I knew the first day. I just *knew* it was not going to work out. And I have known that for two years."

Now two years may be somewhat extreme, but I hear many of my clients report they hired someone, knew they were not going to work out almost immediately, then left the person in the position for months, if not years— just to avoid having to interview again.

I challenge all fellow business owners to hire differently by really *listening* to the candidates during the interviews. They will tell you if they will not work out as your next employee. You just have to listen. For example, last week, I interviewed a candidate that my client really wanted to hire until we started talking about the language this person used in the interview. It was always someone else's fault, they didn't get enough training, and the traffic was always terrible. The client looked at me with this hang dog look, like I had just burst his bubble.

I commented, "Do you know this one is a no?"

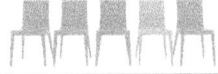

He said, "Yes. But I don't want to know that it's a no. I want a new employee!"

This is the absolute most difficult part of the interview process. You are tired, you need help and you want this person to work out so bad! But as another client of mine said, "When you shorten this process, you pay the piper." And he's right. The price is an employee who you knew from the start would not work out. Then you have to go through the pain of firing and hiring all over again. I encourage you to listen to yourself and the language of your potential new hires. You know when it's a no. Wait until you know it's a yes.

Power Thought

Paying the price in the short term will
reap great benefits in the long run.

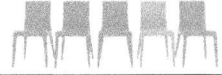

James "Doc" Councilman, swim coach to the great Mark Spitz, was the oldest person to swim across the English Channel at the age of 58. What makes this story so remarkable? He had been diagnosed with Parkinson's disease four years prior. In order to prepare for that amazing swim, he sat in ice cube baths to prepare for the cold water. When reporters asked about his pain level upon his completion, he said, "It only hurt once ... from beginning to end."

Last week, my client and I hired a fabulous candidate, a job well done. We interviewed 38 people, had over 100 applicants, then we ran into wall after wall. We had multiple no-shows, offered the job to someone who couldn't take it, and had someone walk out without shaking our out stretched hands. Upon our glorious candidate accepting the job, my client turned to me and said, "Is there any way you can make this process less painful?" The simple answer is no. I wish I could.

Frankly, the interviewing process is not the most enjoyable business activity. Hence the reason businesses often put it off until the need for someone is so great that they have to begin the interview process. There will be days when you truly despise the process and even me as your interviewing coach. What you will get when you work with me is that I make your life so much easier *after* you go through this process and *after* we find the A-list new hire you are seeking. You will be able to take days off. You will be able to rest. You will be able to trust that things get done. And you will hurt a lot less once you swim that channel. Just like Doc said, "It will only hurt once ... from beginning to end."

Power Thought
No pain, no gain. It's that simple.

I received a phone call from a frantic client who had to fire someone. She was late, she was dropping balls, and worst of all, there had been multiple client complaints. He tried everything that he could to get her up to speed: he sent her to training classes; he moved her office into his; he wrote list after list of processes so that she could learn... nothing worked. After 2 years, it was time to let her go. My client was horrified to take this action. He kept saying how nice she was, what a good person she was, and how much he liked her. Yet, she wasn't getting the job done. He was doing her job *and* his, all the while paying her to do a job not well done.

Here is the bottom line: if someone isn't successful in their job, they aren't happy. If they aren't happy, they aren't successful. They have to *love* their job to be good at it. If they aren't good at it, then everyone loses. Your job as their manager is to recognize when someone isn't being successful, and do everything that you can to help them be successful. If that doesn't work, you need to let them go. You deserve an employee who loves working for you, and your fired employee deserves a chance at happiness. If it isn't working for you, then it isn't working for them either. What I really appreciate about this client is that he isn't excited about firing this person. He isn't making this decision lightly, and it doesn't feel good to him. This time, we will hire the right fit by going through the A-list Interviews 7 Step Process, so that this doesn't happen again.

Power Thought

Correcting a wrong is always the right thing to do.

As most of you know, I foster dogs through a wonderful organization called PawsCo. Our job as fosters is to transition the dog from a shelter environment, an unfit home or an otherwise bad situation. Our last dog was an adorable little dachshund mix with a blond scruffy coat. She is a lap dog in the house, sweet and gentle, but outside? She turns into Devil Dog. She growls at cyclists, cars, wheelchairs, and strollers. She is aggressive and threatening when she is surprised by an oncoming object. At PawsCo, we have access to a wonderful trainer named Megan Hill, who helped us train Chloe by what she calls a "waterfall of treats." Being outside made Chloe very anxious, because she was found on a highway wandering around. In order to survive, she had to be aggressive. Our job is to teach her that being outside is fun and safe. We now go outside and start giving her treats for no reason … just for being outside. Then, we start tapering off, and give her treats any time that we see a car or anything else that makes her growl. We then taper off the treats until she can walk outside without growling and feeling anxious.

The same process occurs when you bring a new employee into your organization. You don't use treats, you use accessibility. Most of my clients think their job is over when we hire someone, but really, *their* job is just beginning. Each employee must be taught their job. No one walks into a position and knows how to do it to your satisfaction without your guidance and input. Be available, be accessible, and check on your new employee often. As they become more confident in their role, you can back off. You can then stick your head in their office and ask how they are doing. Ask how you can help. Ask what questions they have for you. Your commitment to their training will benefit you in ways that you can't know right now, but in the future? You have *hired and trained* your A-list candidate—the one that has your back and performs amazing things for you and your company.

As for Chloe, she was adopted by a wonderful couple. They go on walks with a lot of treats, while she is adapting well to her new environment and loving every minute of it. And we are getting the house ready for our next beloved dog. Happy training!

Power Thought

A guiding hand and an open-door policy are the perfect recipe for success.

My daughter once made a Christmas present for me that she didn't want me to see. She had me bend down and she covered my eyes with her little hands. We stumbled along until we got to her room, then she pulled her hands away. My surprise was a diorama of Christmas at the Smith house, complete with the tree, presents, the stockings by the fireplace and my kid walking in on Santa going up the chimney. It is the cutest thing, and the detail was something that I never would have expected. It sits out on our bookshelf all year round, and I still remember covering my eyes and going in blind to that great surprise.

When I begin working with a new client, I ask them to do something they have never done before: go into an interview with a candidate, blind. Don't read the resume. My client will know the candidate's first name and that is it. Why? Because reading the resume before you meet the candidate gives you the ability to pre-judge. It feeds into our prejudices, and when you read a resume, you miss the surprise. At A-list, we have a person in charge of screening resumes, and he is amazing at it! He developed a process for screening quickly and effectively, all the while, allowing my clients to be surprised by what the candidate brings to the table and checking their prejudices at the door. This process allows for more diversity, more ideas and more creativity in a company.

Next time you hire someone, have someone else screen for you. Don't look at the resumes; be surprised by going in blind into your next interview.

Power Thought
When you don't have preconceived ideas,
you can see and hear so much more.

When my clients have to hire someone, most of them have what I call the "eds":

"The interview I dread

My feet feel like lead

I want to go to bed and

Pull the covers over my head."

When you bring that type of energy to the interview process, guess what type of person you are going to hire? An "ed."

My job is to get my clients to the "ongs":

"I feel powerful and strong

Even when the process is long

That I will find the one

That truly belongs."

Are you ready for an "ong"? Then, you are singing my song!

Power Thought

What you believe to be true, you draw others to. Wahoo!

When I owned my restaurant, we would have really busy times, and I would jump behind the counter and help my staff serve our customers. I was notorious for making margaritas by the bucket. I would go into the basement, get out the tequila, lime juice, triple sec, and apple juice (our secret ingredient) and literally create buckets of margaritas to serve with our amazing enchiladas and nachos. While my staff was thrilled to have me help them get our customers served as quickly as possible, it was a short-term fix to a much larger issue. Whenever we would get hit with a rush of people, as the owner of the company, my time was *not* best served by helping out my staff in the moment. My time was best served by getting more staff on the floor to help the customers get their orders efficiently. In other words, I needed to focus on the bigger picture: Why we were short-staffed at all in that moment.

Three years into owning the restaurant, I quit making margaritas. I refused to step back behind the bar to help, but instead I would begin calling other staff to get more people on the floor. When I hired a general manager, it became his job to make those calls, and my job was to make sure that we had enough staff trained and ready to go for the busy times.

I see this all the time with my clients. They spend their time doing the extra work when they should be spending time looking at the business as a whole. In other words, make your margaritas on Saturday, and focus on your entire business during the week. ¡Olé!

Power Thought

Never lose sight of the big picture by making margaritas.
Delegate to someone who makes them better than you.

As animal fosters, our job is to bring dogs into our home and get them ready for their new forever home by loving them, feeding them, and playing with them. It is such a fulfilling and satisfying way that my family gives back. Other people view fostering differently. There was one woman who wanted to volunteer. She stated up front that she would "only foster dogs with a certain snout," and currently she has never fostered a dog.

I have some people that want to discuss their hiring with me, who present similar requests. They will only work with people who attended a certain university. They will only hire people with a certain GPA. They will only have staff members who are members of certain organizations. And to what avail? The organization that we foster through has a policy of not discriminating against people who want a dog. You don't have to have a white picket fence and a doggy door to adopt a dog; you just have to provide a loving home.

At A-list, we also do not discriminate against clients or job candidates; you just have to want to hire the best fit possible or you have to *be* the best fit for the job. The ultimate irony is that I have hired diverse people from 17-85 years of age, from varying backgrounds, because we focus on three things: working well with others, ability to do the job and passion for the job. Nothing else matters. And the volunteer who wants only dogs with certain snouts? She probably won't foster. The employers who wanted certain GPA's? Statistically, they won't be happy with their hire.

I don't work with people who want certain noses; I work with clients who want to have the best person on their staff and are willing to look past noses in order to find them.

Power Thought

An open mind will open doors of opportunities; a narrow mind will close them. Don't look down your nose!

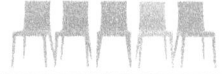

One summer when we were at the beach, my daughter left our condo and forgot her key. I threw on some flip flops, and ran out the door to catch up to her, keys in hand. When I got on the elevator and looked down, I realized that I had one black flip flop on and one blue flip flop on ... it was so funny!

What isn't funny is when you rush through the hiring process, and you get a person who just doesn't match your company's culture. What is painful is when you know on someone's first day that they just aren't going to work out to your satisfaction. What doesn't sit well is when you need one type of shoe, but you put on another. There is a saying: "Hire slow and Fire fast," but nobody does that. We are in too much of a hurry to put a butt in a seat. We think the world will end if we don't hire someone by the end of the week. Really though, what counts is making sure that your flip flops match and that you don't put someone in a position for which they aren't trained, aren't passionate, or don't like. Next time you hire someone, check in the mirror one last time and ensure that your flip flops match. You won't be sorry that you took your time.

Power Thought

Taking a second glance before you step out is
always worth the time.

Rebuttal: How to Spot a Resume of a Psychopath

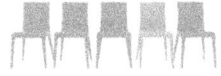

I am sometimes astounded by the amount of misinformation available about how to conduct a good interview and spot an ideal candidate. As I was reading an article by Kathryn Tuggle,[1] I was stunned by the outdated ideas that were presented as benchmarks when determining your next employee. Many of her ideas could actually cause you to *miss out* on a great candidate, with the first problem beginning with the title of the article.

First of all, *no one* can spot a psychopath by reading their resume. As a matter of fact, you can't find a great candidate at all by reading their resume. People on paper are not the same as they are in person. A complete measure of an individual candidate can only occur when you meet face to face.

Second, the article continues to pose that a candidate you are hiring is someone who works "with" you; you are hiring a person to work "for" you. There is an enormous difference in looking for a partner to work "with" and an employee who will work "for" you.

Then, there is the myth of job hopping. The idea that job hopping is a negative is one that we should stop measuring our candidates by. The concept should have gone out with the 1950s notion that you should work for one company until you retire. We have discovered having the same position for decades that lingers on and on (like a bad hangover) actually reduces productivity. Research shows that people who change jobs every two-to-three years are actually more successful.

Ms. Tuggle quoted a psychologist who says that psychopaths will job hop. Well so do people in their 20s who haven't settled down yet. As well as those that realize opportunities may exist more quickly with other companies than a current position may hold. It doesn't mean they are a bad hire. In addition, I greatly appreciate a person who leaves a job because they know it isn't a good fit versus one who will stay just to be able to put two years on a resume. Neither of these situations is a win-win for the employee and the employer. Also, Dr. Greenberg makes the assumption that someone who leaves before a year "can't hold down a job." What if they had to move home to take care of an aging parent? What

---

1   https://www.thestreet.com/personal-finance/how-to-spot-the-resume-of-a-psychopath-applying-to-work-with-you-12927532

if their military spouse got transferred to another state? You *never* know why someone left a job and to assume that they left because they are a psychopath is dangerous and judgmental.

Dr. Greenberg continues to express a concern and assumption that a clear sign of a psychopath is they are unable to be quiet in an interview. Being a talker doesn't mean your candidate is a psychopath. In a well-run interview, the candidate should be talking most of the time and about themselves. They should be letting you know how they can help you, which is not the same as them "blowing their horn for an hour" as referred to in the article. One point that was brought up that I may agree with a bit is when you hear a candidate blaming their boss for not getting promoted. This could be a clear sign that the candidate isn't taking ownership for their part in the last position not working out. Again, that doesn't make the candidate a psychopath. It could just mean the candidate hasn't worked out their issues with the last position. An experienced interviewer will be able to glean enough information from that person to decide if the issues are big enough to warrant not making a job offer.

The last point that Dr. Greenberg makes is that a candidate who compliments you on your office décor is a manipulator. Not necessarily true. They may be trying to break the ice. Interviewing, especially for the candidate, is like no other interaction we experience. If the compliment feels insincere or "slimy" certainly pay attention. However not all people who compliment the interviewer are manipulators.

Articles like these are dangerous. They make broad, sweeping arguments that a particular behavior is bad and that the person exhibiting the behavior is bad. I have successful exceptions to every one of these so called "psychopathic behaviors". Dr. Greenberg needs to stick to therapy and stay out of interviewing.

Power Thought

Listen to what others have to say but be prepared to make
your own judgements.

The single most beautiful resume I have ever seen was written by a woman who stood up at the end of the interview and screamed at my seven-person interview team while banging her fist on the table, "I am not finished telling you about myself!" We had her escorted off the property by security.

The system of screening candidates is backwards. We spend time within the application process by meticulously reviewing resumes when we are really better off spending our time in the interviewing process. Why don't we?

Our culture has told us we can effectively screen people by reading resumes. This is not correct. A resume is simply a marketing piece for the candidate. If a sales person brought a brochure, we would read the fine print. We would ask ourselves, *What is the catch?* If interested, we would call the salesperson and ask questions, but we wouldn't take the marketing piece at face value. So why do we in screening resumes?

People on paper aren't the same as people in person. Randy Smith, A-list Interviews Resume Reviewer Extraordinaire and head of our Application Services, says that the better someone looks on paper, the worse they are in person. I think he's onto something.

If you have ever worked with me in finding your next A-list employee, you went in blind to an interview without looking at resumes of the candidates you are interviewing. My clients have said that *not* looking at resumes before an interview actually allows them focus on the person in front of them. They listen to the candidate, and the candidate gets a more genuine experience with the company. My best advice is to spend your time interviewing, not reviewing resumes in order to find your next best employee. You will be amazed at the difference it makes in finding the ideal person for the job.

Power Thought

Give people your undivided attention in an interview and
you'll be amazed at what you see and hear.

During the World Series of Poker, there was a gentleman who made it to the final table and was the first person to lose. He came in 9th place. The next year the same gentleman made it to the final table where he tweeted to his network "Not going to get 9th place again." Guess what happened? He came in 9th place again. By the way, the chances of a person getting 9th place two years in a row at the World Series of Poker is one in 42 million.

Many of my clients will call me and say they aren't getting the right candidates to the table. I ask them to tell me what their job ad says. I am always a little taken aback by the negative language that people use, i.e., "If you can't be on time, don't apply." I guarantee that when candidates read that line, they see "if you can't be on time, *apply*." And they do!

If you truly want to transform the candidate pool, change your language. Begin by asking for what you want, not what you don't. Then share your mission statement and talk about *why* you are in the business you are in. Simon Sinek wrote a book and shared a TED talk called *Start With Why* that describes fierce loyalty and invested interest when people understand why you do business. Write about the people that you help and how the position will impact them. Describe the position and how it will contribute to the organization, your staff and your clients. If you want to win the game of staffing, then ask for the A-list candidates that you desire and leave 9th place in the dust!

I'm all in!

Are you?

Power Thought

Know why you are the right company and
you will hire the right people.

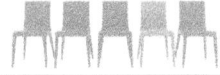

I was recently flying back from Kansas City and was seated behind three gentlemen on a business trip. One of the men was the manager and the other two worked for him. I always like to listen in on conversations between employers and employees as I learn a tremendous amount through their interactions with one another, particularly when it comes to company culture. Here is a recounting of the conversation I overheard:

Manger on the phone: "I'll call you when I get there. Bye honey!"

Employee #1: "You didn't tell your wife what we were doing, did you?"

Boss: "Of course! I don't lie to my wife."

Employee #2 (laughing): "You just color the truth, right?"

Boss: "Nah. She sees through that crap. One of the things that I like about her. Now about those reports … ."

After that, the three men continued to laugh, joke around and talk about business, but the tone of the conversation had shifted. The boss had declared the values of his interaction with his wife and set the tone for the interaction with his employees. This short, simple conversation with the man's wife had shifted the company culture. There is no longer the expectation that you lie to your wife (or to your employer for that matter). The boss declared that lying was unacceptable, and the employees paid attention.

I have many people ask me how to interview more effectively because they want a different company culture. My answer to them is always the same: shifting the culture is a simple conversation about values. Once you know your company values and can articulate them quickly, you have changed your company culture. At A-list Interviews, our values are spelled out through an acronym of "A-list":

A – Authentic

L – Leadership

I – Integrity

S – Satisfaction

T – Teamwork.

Where that culture really plays out is when we make a mistake, we take full responsibility for it. And we certainly don't lie to our spouses (or employees) about it. If you want better culture, set the tone and your people will follow.

Power Thought

Culture attracts and turns away particular types of people.

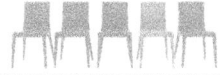

While working with an interview team of six people, I asked them what they thought about a particular candidate, and one by one they all said, "I like him, but ... ."

I then asked, "What's *like* got to do with it?" We all laughed.

Remember, my theory is to go with your "but" not your gut. When you hire someone to work for you, you really don't have to like them. You have to trust that the work will get done. You have to have faith that your clients will be well-cared for and their needs will be met. You have to be able to walk out the door and know that your new hire will have your back. But like them? That's just a bonus.

Why is it that when we interview someone we begin with *like*? Because we don't know how else to evaluate a person. When we meet someone for the first time in our personal lives, we look for similarities and common ground. We look for people like us with the same interests. When we hire someone, we look for a person who can and will do the job that we need for them to do. These are two very different mindsets. Next time you interview someone, don't ask yourself if you like them. Ask yourself if the work will get done effectively and efficiently. Ask yourself if your clients will be happy with this person. Ask yourself if you can leave your company and know they have your back. If you have resounding yeses on all three questions, then hire that person, whether you like them or not.

Power Thought

When someone performs well, you will learn to *love* that person,
even if you don't like them.

One Christmas, my beloved grandmother sent us a 750-piece puzzle with a picture of puppies with different color bows and colorful wrapped presents in the background. Katy and I gathered around the coffee table and hardly got up for three straight days. We began with the outline of the puzzle, filled in the colorful gifts, the bows, and finally the puppies who were all tan. It was so satisfying when we were finished with it!

Completing a puzzle is like completing the 7-steps-to-finding-great-employees interview process. You begin with an outline of what you are looking for, and as you interview more people, the picture of your very best fit begins to fill in the middle. There are times that you get frustrated, and there are times that you get a string of pieces that all fit in at once, and you are so proud! There are times that you look at the same piece a 1000 times before you are able to put it where it belongs. Overall, at the end of the interview process, you should feel like you won the lottery, not like you finished the puzzle but piece number 750 is missing.

The journey of putting your puzzle together is fraught with detours, bumps and bruises, but in the end, it is so completely satisfying when it all comes together. This feeling is precisely why I do every day what I do. I love it!

Power Thought

You can be satisfied with "a piece missing," or you can be fulfilled by seeing the whole puzzle come together.

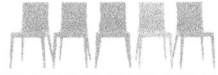

I have not truly relaxed since 1978. In fact, I hate that word! The word "relax" in the same sentence with my name seems like an oxymoron. I am wrapped tight and proud of it!

Imagine my dismay when my swim coach said to me, "Beth, you are going to have to relax in the water." What? This makes no sense! How do you go fast in the water and relax at the same time? When I asked my swim coach this question, he responded, "You let the water move you. Feel it supporting you." Wait ... what?

After some consideration and time trying to reconcile this with my logical brain, I just surrendered to the concept and we began working on relaxing in the water. Much to my surprise, my coach was right! Once I began to relax into my swimming instead of pushing my performance, I actually moved more efficiently in the water with less effort, cutting 15 seconds off my 100-yard freestyle, and 11 seconds off my 100-yard backstroke.

While this life lesson was being presented to me, I realized that if I could encourage my clients to relax during the interview process, we might have similar results. I said to one of my clients that he might think about relaxing while we are in the interview process. He looked at me like I had grown a third eye, but agreed to try. The result I observed was the interview process began to truly work *for* us and allowed the next amazing hire to come to the table faster, just like my swimming. When the person showed up, it was much easier to identify them!

I will keep working on relaxing in the water to improve my swimming. I encourage you to relax during the interview process to increase the likelihood of finding the right people for your team.

Power Thought

Taking a few moments to relax will greatly affect your
ability to see, hear, and understand.

I used to think I hated sushi. I thought, *Who on earth would willingly put raw fish in their mouth, swallow and like it?!* I held strong to this belief until a guy asked me out on a date and took me to my first sushi restaurant. I had no idea how to order, what to do, how to eat and how to use chopsticks, so he showed me how. He ordered very mild fish, because he did not want to turn me off of sushi. He wrapped a rubber band around my chop sticks so that I could learn how to hold them, and he showed me how to mix the wasabi in with the soy sauce so that I didn't destroy my nostrils. That night changed my life ... I fell in love with sushi!

During this amazing night, I also realized I learned an important life lesson as well. The fact is, I could have learned about sushi on my own. I could have struggled with my chopsticks and put *way* too much wasabi in my soy, but I had a guide; someone to show me the ropes, so that my experience was so much more enhanced and the likelihood that I would actually enjoy sushi was increased.

How does this apply to business? I realized early in my professional career that I could teach myself certain skills and muddle through all of the mistakes that come from learning a new skill set. I also realized there are times when it is better to have a guide, a professional who can lead me through the learning curve, increasing the likelihood I would both like the activity and increase my effectiveness when executing it.

At A-list Interviews, I am your guide in interviewing for new employees. Can you do it yourself? Yes. Should you? Eventually. Having someone in your corner with an objective opinion acting on your behalf and showing you the way will definitely enhance your experience. Hire all you want, when you want, but hire an expert to be your guide. You deserve it!

Power Thought

Everyone who succeeds has someone in their corner.

In a recent interview, we asked candidates some questions about project management. One candidate was talking about how their part of a project was completed even though their boss's portion had not been finished. I said to the potential employee, "What would you do should this happen again?"

Without missing a beat, he said, "I'd chew her out. Just joking!"

After the interview was over, I said to my client, "You know that we cannot hire that candidate based on that statement."

The client responded, "But he was just joking, Beth."

I replied, "Maybe so, but chewing out your boss? That's not funny."

In an interview, our job as hiring managers is to listen actively to the exact words of the candidate's response. Remember, a job seeker will attempt to put their very best foot forward to impress a potential employer. If you listen to the actual language they are using within their finely-tuned responses, you can identify personality traits and core values around work. Through this knowledge, you can identify how a person will fit into your culture, what type of management style they will thrive under and more. Therefore, if you are going to listen to the candidate's "just joking" comment, then you also have to pay attention to the "chewing out" part.

When we are conducting interviews, we tend to listen to what we *want* to hear because we want to hire someone. We want the candidates to succeed and become our next new employee! And we are often willing to do whatever it takes to *make* the candidate ideal, including dismissing a comment like "just joking." We do not know what the candidate meant when he said that he was just joking. Maybe he was. But maybe he wasn't. Can you take that chance with a critical function like a new hire? If you do take that chance and he was not joking, do you want to work with an employee who will "chew you out?" While it may appear the language being used was positioned as a joke, hiring is no laughing matter.

Power Thought

What people say in an interview is no joke.

At the end of an interview, a candidate asked me, "Can I ask you a fun question?"

"Sure," I responded.

The candidate then asked me, "If you were stranded on a desert island, and you could only have 1 c.d. for your c.d. player, which one would it be?"

I said, "Patsy Cline's greatest hits.

"Awesome," he sighed.

I began to ask myself about the point of his question. Through his question, what did he discover about the company culture? Nothing. What does he now know about the job? Nothing. What information does he now have that he didn't before? None. So, why ask the question?

People are constantly asking me what questions I ask a candidate in an interview, so I tell them. It is no secret. I want to know about your relationship with your past managers and co-workers, how you handle being overwhelmed, and how much research was done on the company for which they are interviewing. These questions all apply to the job. I do not ask about deserted islands, how many golf balls fill an airplane, or if you were a cheese, which one would it be, because those questions cannot be evaluated. Whether you consider yourself as blue cheese or Swiss cheese does not help me determine if you can do the job that I am asking you to do, and if you want to do the job that I am asking you to do. Questions related to Patsy Cline can come later after the person has been hired. And truth be told, I would actually not be listening to Patsy on that island. I would use the c.d. to reflect the sun to a passing airplane so that I could be rescued.

Power Thought

Question your questions,
so that you won't question your decisions.

We all know what we need to do to lose weight. Eat less, work out more. Eat more vegetables and less sugar. Cut out the sodas and too much salt. Cross train in your workouts so that your body is constantly doing different activities. Eat out less and at home more. There are no short cuts. No pills to swallow that lead to long-term weight loss, and no quick fixes. No one can do it for you. You have to do it yourself.

The same could be said for hiring. There are no short cuts or quick fixes. You have to run a strategic process that means you will interview a lot of people. You have to know what you want, and you can never second guess yourself. And, *no one* can do it for you—not even me. While I am considered an expert on the interview process with an average 30-50 people interviewed each week and almost 20,000 people in my career, I still cannot interview *for* you. I can only interview *with* you. I can show you how to prepare, conduct and perform an interview to find the very best people for your team. I can share my expertise with you, but I cannot do it for you. The minute you step away from the process, the effectiveness of your hiring process goes down.

How do you lose weight while interviewing? You eat a spinach salad at lunch and take a quick walk around the building on your break. You leave the cookies in the break room for others to eat, and you do not go into the break room until they are all gone. You drink a ton of water and you keep your eye on the prize—a fantastic new candidate and new pants in a smaller size.

Power Thought

When all is said and done, you are completely responsible
... and that's a good feeling.

I recently got a new/used car, and at the end of a long day of interviewing, I got in it to go home. It has one of those keyless buttons that you press to make it start (this is new technology to me). I pushed the button and ... nothing. I began to try everything I could think of to get the vehicle to start. I discovered the "key" in the key fob where I turned the car off, then on again. I opened and shut all the doors. Nothing happened.

One of the employees who was leaving at the same time offered, "Beth, do you need some jumper cables? I don't have any, but I could call somebody!"

I gracefully declined. Even if she had jumper cables, I would not have known what to do with them; and I was pretty sure the issue with the car was user error, not engine failure. As I continued my discovery process— which involved me sitting in the front seat staring out the window in amazement, hoping a solution would just present itself—my client walked by and said, "Is the car in park?"

The car was in reverse.

I put the car in park and it started right up at the push of the button. Boy, did I feel like an idiot, and I can guarantee you that I have not heard the end of this from my client or friends, nor will I ever! It was such a simple fix.

"What is the point?" you might be asking. Last week, an article[1] came out about a tech company failing to attract female candidates. After some conversations, they realized the job title they'd used for years ("hacker") was not perceived as inclusive by potential candidates. Once they changed their verbiage from "hacker" to "developer," they began to attract many more female candidates. Sometimes a very simple change (in this case, of one word) can make all the difference in the world.

---

[1]   https://open.bufferapp.com/job-descriptions-diversity

The next time you find yourself not attracting the types of candidates that you want (or when your new/used car will not start), take a second look. Put your process (and car) in park. Take a second to review your job ad to ensure that the language you are using directly reflects the message you want to portray. Then, press the button and GO! Meanwhile, I will be reading the manual for my car... .

Power Thought

Before all else fails, read the instructions;
you will save yourself time and frustration.

"I pruned a tree once, so technically I'm allowed
to put 'branch manager' on my resumé."

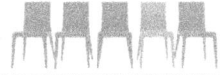

I love the salad bar at Whole Foods! I mean, I *love* it! It is a luxury that I rarely allow myself, but I will eat vegetables there that I would never eat at home. I love having the ability to choose which high quality ingredients go into my salad, and my mouth just waters. I get excited just by thinking about it, because I know that it will be the best salad I have had in a long time.

What would it be like if you could choose your next employee that way? What if you could hand pick the qualities of your potential candidate the way you can the vegetables at a salad bar? What if you walked around the "candidate" bar and were able to choose the qualities in a great employee that got you excited? For example, pick up the tongs over the "Loves Coming to Work" container, or pass over the "Can't See the Big Picture" container. After all, if you don't like mushrooms, you don't put them in your salad! It will just ruin your experience.

In essence, it really is that easy if you have a strategic interviewing process in place. You begin with the Ideal Candidate List (step one in the A-list Interview process). Make a list of all the qualities that make up your Ideal Candidate and post that list on your wall. Look at it every day, and continue interviewing until you find that person. Then your new employee experience will be just like going to Whole Foods and walking around the salad bar: exciting, full of anticipation and a wholly satisfying, memorable experience.

Power Thought

The right hire is just as satisfying to your company as a
great meal is to you.

Imagine being in an interview for a job that you really want. The interview team is a panel of people who are not doing all the talking, but asking you pretty hard questions, and you are concentrating solely on impressing them. All of the sudden, one of those people points out that you have a spider crawling on your shirt. What would you do? Would you scream? Jump up and run? Brush that spider off and then kill it *dead*?

This actually happened to a poor candidate that we interviewed, and he calmly brushed the spider off his shirt and continued his interview gracefully. Then, he joked about being Peter Parker. We all laughed uproariously. He followed up later that day with a thank you email for the opportunity to interview, expressed his desire to come back for the final round as he really wanted this job, and he signed his email: "Your friendly neighborhood spider man."

I have spent hours talking to my clients about what to look for in candidates, and the ability to handle difficult situations is invariably one of the top qualities that my clients want. An employee who can laugh at themselves and the situation, handle it gracefully and leave you impressed in an awkward set of circumstances is someone you have to hire. And as for Spiderman? He was hired for ... you guessed it, a web developer.

Power Thought

We all go through tough times—that's life. But how you go
through depends on your ability to see the humor!

While vacationing recently, I took long walks on the beach. The wind in my hair, the sun on my face, the sand under my toes ... pure bliss. After a few days, I began to look around at the other folks enjoying their time on the beach as well. What I noticed was shocking—not a single person was on their phone. I didn't see a soul on an iPad. I didn't even see a Kindle. What I did see was people talking to each other. I saw people playing games together and building sand castles with their kids. I saw people napping, eating, reading and working. Yes, I did say *working*.

After sitting on the beach for a while, your mind wanders. You look around to see the surroundings and, lo and behold, inspiration strikes. People made some of the most beautiful sand castles, wrote inspirational messages in the sand, collected sea shells and created artwork. They were *working*. The word "work" means "an activity involving mental or physical effort done in order to achieve a purpose or result." And at the end of the day, people were satisfied. Work has literally become a four-letter word, something that we have to endure in order to live.

I think work is a beach. When we are inspired by our work, we create and innovate. We are more willing to try new things, and we sometimes make mistakes. We are learning! If you are thinking to yourself, "Work is a bi*%h," then I encourage you to visit a beach—stat!

Power Thought

When and where are you at your creative best?
Spend more time there.

One dreary Monday morning, a friend of mine dragged himself into work. Sighing deeply, he prayed that his enormous coffee would somehow get him through the worst time of the week—the weekly staff meeting. Boring! This week, however, his manager came in and dumped a huge bucket of Legos on the table. He grabbed the flat green stand, attached three Legos to it, and turned to the employee sitting to his right and said, "Take three Legos, add it to mine, then pass it to the next person. Let's see what we can create." Then, the manager went on with the regular staff meeting. Same format, same information, but the atmosphere had dramatically changed. What the team created was an unnamable, indescribable Lego blob, and a whole lot of laughter on a dreary Monday morning.

My friend bounced back to his desk with a spring in his step that had nothing to do with his huge cup of coffee. What transpired after that was fantastic! The team got closer, created more, cooperated more and laughed at inside jokes around the Lego disasters that came out of those meetings. It then became the responsibility for other team members to bring an activity to the staff meeting. However, what really mattered was the manager got his team out of the rut they were in, and suddenly there was a huge shift in energy and innovation.

If you are the manager of a team and you dread your own meetings, then certainly your employees dread it as well. Take a moment to figure out how to get yourself out of the rut, then provide a cure for the interminable dreaded staff meeting. A little playtime does wonders.

Power Thought

Ruts are for people who play it safe. If you want innovation, introduce play time at work.

While I addressed this earlier, lately I have seen several articles about how to win the so-called "Talent War," and I just can't stay quiet!

Folks, *there is no Talent War*!

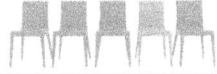

This is a fear-based myth created by someone who doesn't like recruiting. Are there candidates who are not qualified that apply for your position? Yes. Are there people who walk into an interview and you *know* that you wouldn't hire them to walk you across the street? Yes. Do you have horror stories about interviewing people? Oh gosh yes!

But then, after you have gone through the sometimes-arduous interview process that feels like a war, you meet the one! The person who comes in and owns your job like they were born to be there. The one who makes your job easy because they have your back and are capable and invested in their role within the organization. The single employee who within minutes makes you realize that you have a gem, and you are suddenly so excited to get out there and do your real job! There are seven billion people on this earth, more people than ever in history, and you just need *the one*.

The problem is not lack of talent; it is lack of an interview process to find that right person. Your person is out there somewhere, and they are looking for you; you just need the patience and the process to find them.

Power Thought

Recruiting is not a war zone; it's a "seeing potential" and
"what if?" zone.

The Interviewer, the Client and the Bridesmaid

Recently, my client and I called a candidate to get her scheduled for an interview. The candidate asked for a phone interview at noon on the Friday afternoon that we had available. She was very specific about the time. When I asked her if there was a reason, she responded, "Yes. I am in a wedding that day and it starts at 2:00." Since we schedule phone interviews all the time, I asked her if another day and time might be better. She replied, "No, I do not want to miss out on this opportunity."

On the day of her interview, I asked her if she was ready for the wedding, and she said, "Yes. We have done our hair and makeup, and I am sitting in a church pew in my Bridesmaid's dress. This is a first for me."

It was a first for me and the client as well! The most amazing part about that interview wasn't the dress or dedication to taking the call, although these were great steps to showing her enthusiasm for the position; it was actually in her preparation. She had conducted her research on the company. She referred to Yelp reviews. She asked excellent questions and she referred to her "list" of questions several times. She knocked the ball out of the park—all in her bridesmaid dress.

Brilliant. Truly brilliant.

Power Thought
Prior preparation prevents poor performance.

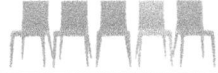

Back in the 1950s, many vacuum cleaners were sold door-to-door. A salesman would come to the home and be invited into stage a demonstration of the vacuum's effectiveness. Usually, that demonstration involved dumping dirt and debris on the carpet and then using the vacuum to remove it. But what happened if the vacuum didn't suck up the dirt? The homeowners were left with a mess in the middle of their living room. (And of course, they did not buy the vacuum.)

Surprisingly, people today often use the job interview as an opportunity to dump unwanted "dirt and debris" all over the conference table. Candidates report how awful their past employers were, how horrible their last job was and how impossible the boss was to please. Last week, a candidate complained to me that he had "embellished" his skills when applying for his previous position and was subsequently fired. His exact quote was, "If they had just *trained* me on those skills (that he already told the boss he had), then I could have been successful."

Just like a non-working vacuum, if there is a big pile of "dirt and debris" sitting on the conference table after an interview, then the candidate isn't the right fit for your organization. Clean up the dirt, and keep searching for the right candidate.

Power Thought

Don't allow a candidate to dump dirt in an interview.
That makes your whole place dirty.

The question that every client invariably will ask me when we begin to develop their interviewing process is, "Why can't I hire good people?" My poor clients are often doing their full-time jobs along with the full-time jobs of other employees. My clients are tired, burned out, and can hate the work they do because they need good help and are feeling overwhelmed.

One client confessed to me that he hated going into the office every day, because his direct reports will have put piles of work on his desk that ultimately belonged on their own desks. "Beth, why can't I hire good people?" he asked.

My answer? Because you don't need good *people*. You need good *employees*. There is a big difference. Think of it this way: I consider myself a good person. I vote, I recycle, I save dogs and I take good care of my clients. I hold the doors open for people, and I honestly care about our planet. Like I said, a good person. But if you put me in front of a computer for 50 hours a week with a set of headphones doing internet research, I would lose my mind! I would become a lunatic with a road rage problem! A good person, but a terrible employee, because I am in the wrong job. I need to be with people, working with people, talking to people, or I am not happy or productive.

Hiring good employees means that you hire people because they are in the right job. Hiring good people and putting them in a job they hate makes them bad employees. My advice: Do not hire good people, hire good employees.

Power Thought

Good employees are always good people.
Good people are not always good employees.

Do you walk into your office and see zombies disguised as employees? Those lifeless bodies that wander around thoughtlessly in packs? Have you ever thought about how they got that way?

New employees are always so excited to start their job. I have heard many new hires talk about their first day on the job just like they talk about their first day of school, with excitement and awe. How is it that years or even months into their employment with a company, these same enthusiastic people lose their passion for the job?

Because we suck the life out of them with too many constraints and not enough direction.

We make it hard for them to do their jobs with petty rules. We don't spend enough time training new people, and we really don't take the time to explain our expectations. All of the sudden, we have a lifeless body in place of the previously excited employee.

If you look around and see zombies on your staff, it is time to take stock of your interviewing process, your training program, *and* your employee handbook. If you are dictating when someone can go to the bathroom, you are running a daycare, not a professional office. It is time for a re-do. And if that doesn't work, try chocolate!

Power Thought

Empower your employees to work to their
fullest potential.

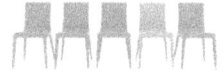

I was interviewing with a client who turned to me and said, "Beth, I am so sick of interviewing people!"

I responded, "Well, you better learn to love it."

He looked horrified, and asked, "Why?"

"Because if you are going to grow and evolve as a company, you will be constantly interviewing people," I replied.

My answer made him feel a little sick. This mindset of hating interviewing is common among many of my clients. They *hate* interviewing. They *hate* spending all day sitting in a room with a steady stream of people coming through the building. They *hate* "wasting time" and not being able to do their "real job."

Here is the truth. When you run a company or department, your job is to create the vision for your area and hire the people who fit that vision. If you approach this valuable activity with any other intention, then you *are* wasting your time. Instead of coming to the table hating the interviewing process, shift to learning how to *love* finding new employees. Begin by getting in touch with the end goal, which is to find an amazing candidate who comes in and knocks the ball out of the park. *That* person will let you go back to doing what you love to do. Hiring the very best fit means that you spend some time interviewing candidates to find employees who love what they do. Then you get to spend more time doing things that you love. You cannot find a better way to spend your time than that.

Power Thought

Begin with the end in mind and
you *will* find who/what you are looking for.

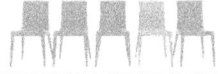

There are some days when I help my clients with interviewing where we speak to people all day only to find no one qualified to move to the next interview. This can be discouraging, but when we understand the importance of finding the right person for the job, we also understand that having no one to move forward is inherent to the process.

After a particularly difficult interview day where this scenario occurred, my client turned to me and said, "I just want to thank you for your hard work and for hanging in there with me. I am really grateful for having you here."

Wow! It is wonderful to work with people who understand we do not always find the right person immediately. When this happens, I'm even more grateful they still see the value of the A-list Interviews process.

As I drove home from the session, I had such a warm glow in my heart and it got me thinking. Do I say "thank you" often enough, even in the face of adversity? I certainly hope so. If you have not heard "thank you" from me recently, I want to express my gratitude now. Some of you on this distribution list are amazing clients; some of you are incredible network partners or even people I have only met once at an event; some of you are people I perhaps have never met. Regardless, I sincerely appreciate your readership, partnership, trust and support over the years for A-list and myself. Each and every one of you has contributed to my success in some way.

Towards the end of the year, I find it timely to remind you all of my gratitude: gratitude for my clients, my vendors, my employees, my family and my friends. And I want to thank all of you. Just as my client reminded me earlier this month that a simple thank you speaks volumes, I now pass it along to you and yours, and please know that I am eternally grateful for you all. Muchas gracias! Merci! Thank you!

Power Thought

Gratitude is a universal language that
everyone understands.

My personal trainer is Christine Neff (a.k.a. Marquis de Sade). She has this wicked sense of humor as she gleefully kicks my butt all over the gym. When I look at her with an evil stare she yells, "Now there is that 'I love you Christine look!" Last week, she made me do push-ups. I hate push-ups because I struggle with them!

One day she told me that the final push-up, the one I only half do is the very best one ... huh? "Your strength comes from the struggle," she said.

Finding the right person to hire is always a struggle, which is why my clients have difficulty with interviewing. You cannot just go online and place a special order for the right fit. You especially cannot get any deals or shortcuts when it comes to finding the right employee. You have to go through the seven-step interview process fully and completely, and yes, you must struggle. The person that you hire out of desperation, out of fear or out of panic will never work out for you. You have to complete the interview process in order to hire the brightest and the best; when you finally do hire, it is so satisfying!

When I met with Christine before Thanksgiving, I was able to finish four-and-a-half complete push-ups! The half push-up was by far the hardest. But with arms shaking and sweating profusely, I struggle and I continue to get stronger. Fist bump!

Power Thought

Through your patience in the process,
you will possess your reward.

Over the Thanksgiving holiday, my daughter Katy and I were listening to the radio. A song came on that we both love. I began belting out the tune at the top of my lungs and sang along to the chorus of the Zac Brown Band song. I sang "Long Gone" along in perfect pitch (to me at least). My kid laughed uproariously.

"Mom," she yelled, "Those aren't the words!"

"Yes they are!" I replied.

She giggled then said, "No, really. It's not Long Gone. It's Home Grown!"

She had to Google it for me to believe her.

This misunderstanding happens in interviews for new employees all the time. Someone on the interview team will recount what the candidate said and someone else will have heard the words completely differently. The very first step in the analysis of an interview for the hiring team is to agree to what the candidate actually said. The actual choice of words they used are very important. For example, "My boss is really great to work with." Did they really say "with"? Are you sure they didn't say, "My boss is really great to work *for*"? That simple word changes the entire meaning of the sentence as well as the intent of the comment. The word "with" denotes that the candidate doesn't acknowledge their manager's authority, and if they don't acknowledge it in the interview, they won't do so when they have direct deposit. I talk about listening to the exact words all the time to my clients to ensure they hire someone who will fit with the company culture, leadership style and even the position itself.

If you are not paying attention, you can miss something really important in an interview, which can lead to a bad hire. You can also really embarrass yourself in front of your teenage daughter.

Power Thought

When you can repeat back what someone has said,
then you have truly heard them.

Grammar, Boys and Resumes

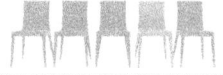

My daughter received a text from a potential suitor that said, "Your so pretty!" Katy showed me the text with a horrified look on her face and said "I'm sorry. If he doesn't know the difference between your/you're and to/two/too, then I am not interested."

In my business, we receive hundreds of resumes for jobs per week and at least half of them have some sort of grammar and/or spelling error. Sometimes we interview the person anyway because they have the experience we are looking for, they wrote a "nice" cover letter or we decide to forgive that "one tiny mistake."

But here is the hard and fast truth: The easiest way to determine if the candidate is serious about the position is whether or not they took the extra two minutes to run spell check and proofread their work. It really isn't hard. It really doesn't take much time. It really does make a difference. For those candidates who are continuously asking me for interviewing help, my best advice to get the interview is to please do a review of your materials *before* you send them. Better yet, have your neighbor, friend or significant other read your resume and cover letter, for an extra set of eyes. And for my clients who ask, yes, grammar counts! Just ask my beloved teenage daughter!

P.S. May all boys within dating age of my daughter make all kinds of grammatical errors. Amen.

Power Thought
Your choice of words speaks volumes about you.

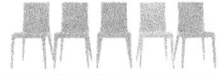

A few years ago, I injured my eye, and the eye doctor said that I could never wear contacts again. What a shock! I wasn't happy about it, but the diagnosis was very clear. I had no choice. I bought a pair of glasses that I really liked, and I never looked back.

However, at a recent annual eye exam, my doctor suggested contacts. I couldn't believe it! Apparently, contacts have dramatically improved, and there was a healthy option for me to now use. I was ecstatic.

Imagine my surprise when I began wearing my new set of contacts and felt like something was missing. I would walk by a mirror and say "Who is *that*?" I noticed that I pushed my no-longer-existing glasses higher on my face several times a day and even poked myself in the eye. I smeared my mascara multiple times, and one time, I put my glasses on *after* I put my contacts in. Oops. My adjustment period after I ditched my spectacles was at best unexpected, and at its worst really uncomfortable. However, now that I am through the transition, I am loving life and seeing clearly!

In business, we expect an adjustment period after an employee leaves. However, the bigger adjustment happens when a new employee starts. Adding someone to your team is a big change that can be awkward, even when you have hired the ideal A-list employee. The adjustment period not only affects you, the new employee, the other employees, clients and vendors. You may even walk by their desk and think "Who is that?" or even poke yourself in the proverbial eye a few times while you all adjust. As the employer, it is your job to make that transition easier for all parties involved. Be patient with yourself and your team. As a result, you will all be able to see more clearly.

Power Thought

When you embrace change,
you "see" a world of possibilities.

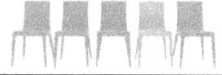

One of my long standing, most beloved clients called wanting to meet with me to discuss some potential new hires for her company. We had not talked in several months, and I was grateful to hear her voice. Over chips and salsa, the conversation started like this:

"Do you remember that woman you interviewed for me four months ago?"

"Vaguely," I replied.

"You told me not to hire her."

"Ummm ... okay," I said, thoroughly confused. If I remembered correctly, the candidate had not been a cultural fit for the rest of her team. I wasn't a part of the actual hiring process for this individual and had instead been invited into evaluate her top three candidate selections.

"Another consultant told me to hire her, so I did." My client sighed deeply, threw her head in her hands and wailed "I am in hell!"

She promptly ordered a margarita and began to tell me the horror stories related to her bad hire.

First, I have such empathy for this woman. There is nothing worse than making a bad hiring decision, then having to watch how it affects the rest of your organization. From employee morale to bottom line results, a bad hire creates turmoil that feels very much like a slap in the face every time you go to work. Second, my best advice to her was to be kind to herself and remind her that some lessons need to be learned despite other people's insights and experiences.

Remember: interviewing and hiring is a skill set and any new skill takes time to learn. You don't just wake up one day knowing how to staff your company. You have to practice, and that means making mistakes. A bad hire is a mistake, and just like any other mistake; learn from it, correct it and move on.

Power Thought
If at first you don't succeed, try, try again.

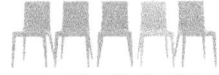

You may recall that a few years ago, my daughter Katy came home with Harley, a fish that she saved from certain death in her science class experiment. Reviewing that saga gave me a great reminder about the power of investing in your employees. I am sad to report that Harley is now swimming in the fishbowl in the sky after a long, productive life at the Smith house ... May he rest in peace.

After the fish bowl was thoroughly drained and cleaned, it sat on our kitchen counter for a few weeks. Finally, I said, "Let's get rid of the fish bowl. There is no reason to have it without a fish in it." Katy's response was noncommittal, so the fish bowl continued to sit on the kitchen counter. I tried again asking, "Should we move the fish bowl?" Still no response. Then out of the blue, Katy said, "Let's get a fish!" and scurried out of the house. One hour later, we had Coby, short for cobalt, a blue betta who is now swimming in the fish bowl on the counter.

All too often, we may need to quickly remove an employee. We tell ourselves that we *must* have that desk filled ASAP, and we frantically start looking for a butt to put in that seat. This can (and often does) lead to poor hiring decisions.

To find the A-list employee that is ideal for the position, there must be space between the previous employee and the new one coming in; the fishbowl must remain empty for a period of time. Don't rush into anything new until you are ready. Take the time to contemplate and explore the options: Maybe you don't need that position any more, or maybe that position should morph into something else. Or maybe, just maybe, it is time to hire the absolute best employee ever! When you give it space and time, you and your team have the opportunity to review the job description, determine the ideal candidate ... and only then begin to search for the next employee.

This blog is dedicated to Harley, who provided hours of entertainment and fodder for my most read blogs. RIP Harley!

Power Thought

Life might be akin to a fish bowl, but not all fish are the
right fit for a particular fish bowl.

Why My 92-Year-Old Grandmother Surpasses Most Candidates

When I flew back to Texas to celebrate my grandmother's 92nd birthday with the entire family, we had a blast! My favorite part of the weekend was the serendipitous hour-long conversation that she and I shared at breakfast. My grandmother made her famous pancakes and little sausages on Saturday morning. My family eagerly poured into seats around her kitchen table to enjoy the best pancakes in the world.

As luck would have it, I slept a little late and was the last one at the table. She sat down with a cup of coffee and we had one of the best conversations we have ever had. My grandmother is articulate, smart, witty and resourceful. She texts friends and family from her iPhone, she is active on Facebook, and she could write a textbook on how to respond to anyone in a sticky situation. She walks every morning and volunteers with her church. She lives by herself, cooks lunch for several of her children most days of the week, and drives herself to the grocery store to shop. At age 92, she remains relevant. I am lucky to have her in my life.

My grandmother, Virginia Ann ("V.A.") Rawlins Littleton, is a class act, possesses excellent customer service skills and knows how to give advice in a way that is easy to accept. If she were a candidate I was interviewing for a position, I'd hire her in a heartbeat.

The next time you begin a job search, please keep in mind that age means nothing when you are looking for the right candidate. There is *always* an exception to every stereotype out there, and V.A. Littleton is not only that exception, in all ways she is exceptional!

Power Thought

Being an exceptional person is a choice that is made on a
daily basis, regardless of age.

My daughter Katy recently attended a baseball game with a group of friends. One of the pitches hit the catcher in the shoulder and bounced off. Katy cried out in alarm, "The squatty dude is hurt!"

Her friend Jorge looked at her in alarm, exclaiming, "Oh Katy!" and threw his head in his hands. He sat up with a deep sigh, and said "What is the squatty dude called?"

"Uhhh ... I don't know."

"The Catcher. What is the guy called who is holding the ball?"

"Uhhh ... the thrower?"

"He is called the pitcher, because all players throw."

"Ohhh," Katy said.

By this point, all of her friends gathered around for Katy's education.

Another friend asked, "What is the name of the guy with the bat?"

"Well, he's the swinger, of course!"

Welcome to spring training! This is what your new employee feels like on their first day of work. Even if they had experience in their particular role in the past, they don't know your company's culture and they don't know some of the terminology and language that your people use. What's more, they don't know the "inside jokes" that come from day-to-day interactions with coworkers and special events with the organization; the new employee barely knows where the bathroom is!

Training a new employee is much more than just showing someone where the files are saved and how to process reports. It's an opportunity to welcome a new person into the fold and show them the best of your organization: to demonstrate the knowledge and experience of your team members and to showcase the bond those people have when they're interacting with each other and doing their jobs.

Bless Katy's friends for filling her in on terms that she didn't know. Yes, they laughed at her, but she laughed right along with them. They formed a bond with each other because her friends took the time to train her.

When Jorge asked her, "Do you know who the Kansas City Royals are?"

She replied (in true Katy fashion), "Of course! They are the baseball team that won the ... uhhh ... really, big game."

Jorge has his work cut out.

Power Thought

When individuals work together in a team environment,
everyone wins.

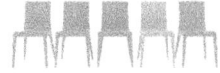

You would think that having a 3.2 percent unemployment rate would be cause for celebration, and it is. Times are good, and there are lots of jobs out there. So, why is it that my clients are afraid they will be unable to find great employees?

Lately, I have received several calls from people who are afraid of the tight labor market. "Where am I going to find good people?" they say. "What if I can't find who I need? The work is overflowing. I need good people!" I hear such comments consistently. The funny thing is that these are the same comments that I heard in 2008 when the job market tanked. Are you surprised? It seems my clients worry about finding the right employee when they have 1000 resumes for one position or 30. They fear that the right person will choose the next company to work for whether they have interviewed 50 candidates or five.

Here is what I tell them: "There are more people on this earth now than ever before. We have seven billion people on this planet, and you need one. The articles that talk about a shortage of candidates are short-sighted and fear-based, and I don't want you to read them anymore. Don't buy into the fear, because when you do you make horrible hiring decisions.

Your job is to stay focused on your search, and the 7 steps to Hiring your A-list Candidate:

1. Create your Ideal Candidate List.
2. Write your amazing job description.
3. Write your job ad leading with the mission statement.
4. Review resumes
5. Interview #1
6. Interview #2
7. Interview # 3.

Hiring in a tight labor market is the same as hiring in an abundant one: Hold out for the right fit. Period.

Power Thought
Stay focused on your goal, not on the distractions.

"I own a universal TV remote, so technically I can call myself a 'multimedia systems coordinator.'"

Coby, the Fishbowl and Employee Resignations

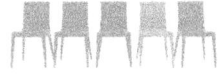

I have written several blogs about Harley, the beta fish that my daughter saved from the wretched science experiment. Recently, I have introduced Coby, our new beloved blue betta. One day, Coby was placed in a small cup while I cleaned out the fish bowl. I had to walk away for a couple of minutes, then came back into the kitchen to finish the job. I couldn't believe my eyes! Coby had leapt out of the cup and was flopping around on the counter and gasping. I sprang into action and saved the fish from certain death ... whew!

When an employee resigns from your organization, there is always a certain level of panic. Even in a situation where the resignation is the best thing for the company, employers worry about the ramifications: Will others leave too? Is this indicative of a larger problem? What will my clients think? How will I get this work done? Should I re-negotiate with this employee in order to retain them?

The urge to spring into action and restore the employee to their position is often a first instinct of an employer, as it was when I found Coby on the counter. Despite first instinct, the two situations couldn't be more different.

My advice for an employer in this predicament is: Help that person leave well. Tell them that you truly appreciate the time they gave to your organization, and ask what they need from you. Figure out a way to let that person make their exit on good terms so that everyone feels better. You are the manager. You set the tone. Give your former employee the freedom to be successful and continue on their own path. You will feel better that you did.

Power Thought

Staying calm and positive in bleak situations is a hallmark
of successful people.

May is a very stressful month for school age kids, no matter what age they are. My daughter Katy is finishing her freshman year, and has finals, final projects, end-of-term tests, make-up work from her surgery, cheerleading practice and many goodbyes to graduating friends. Last week she said, "Mom, I woke up with tears in my eyes today. I knew I wouldn't get through the day without crying, so I made sure to wear waterproof mascara."

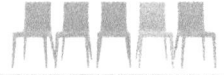

We have a saying around our house that goes like this: "Prior preparation prevents poor performance" and we refer to it as the 5 Ps. Katy woke up, assessed her situation and did something to set herself up for success. Wouldn't it be amazing if your employees did this?

One of my clients had an employee who went on maternity leave and left a long, detailed list with her assistant on what to do for what projects. The leave went great! Business continued and clients were happy. Contrast that experience with another client whose employee took a vacation, during which my client discovered all sorts of work that wasn't done. Their clients were furious, and my client spent the whole week in "clean up" mode. The employee was subsequently fired.

Assessing an employee's ability to be prepared begins in the interview process. Have they done their research on your company? Did they come with a list of questions? Did they attempt to think about themselves in the role? Your A-list hire will be prepared so that you can be prepared. Clients are happy. Business grows. And no one ends up with black smudges on their face.

Power Thought

A project—and a business—lives or dies based on how well an individual or team has prepared.

In a North Carolina children's ballet class recently, the teacher declared the very next practice would be "Princess Day." While all of the other five-year-old little girls whirled and twirled in their beautiful gowns and frilly skirts, wearing tiaras and carrying scepters, little Ainsley came dressed as a hot dog—yes, an All-American Frankfurter hot dog, complete with mustard and a bun. (She also wore her Princess outfit underneath in case she got hot in her truly original hot dog costume.)

Last week, I was talking to a potential new client who confessed, "We just can't find good people!"

"Would you recognize a good candidate if you saw one?" I asked.

"You know, I am really not sure," they said.

Until we start with Step 1 of the A-list Interview Process, many of the clients that I work with have no firm idea what they want in an employee, outside of a certain job-related skill set. Step 1 of our process is called the Ideal List: If you could have anyone that you wanted for this position, who would they be? What would they know? Dream Big! More importantly, we ask the question, "Why do you want what you want?" This process identifies the qualities desired in the ideal candidate, and often reveals quite a bit that wasn't initially apparent. In other words, instead of the princess that you originally thought you wanted, maybe what you really want is a hot dog.

Power Thought
Be open-minded; possibilities come in all shapes and sizes.

You are a badass! is the title of the latest book I have read by Jen Sincero, and every time I read it, pick it up or even just look at it, I think of you. I know that right now you are struggling to find the best employees and it is hard work! Slogging through resumes, interviewing candidates and trying to find the time to do your own job on top of that … and pulling your hair out at the difficulty of the process. After a really bad day of interviewing (or more than one) you say, "Where are all of the good people?" You really want to give up and just hire someone already!

I want you to keep your chin up, because you are a badass! You deserve to have the best of the best, and those people are coming. Get out your Ideal Candidate List and read over it again. Get in touch with how amazing it is going to be when these people finally arrive. When they do—hang onto your hat—you will be floored at the difference they make and you will be thankful that you held your ground and didn't give in to the temptation to just fill an empty chair. In the meantime, when you have a lousy day, look back at how far you have come. Look at the changes you have already made and what a difference it has made on your organization *and* your life. Keep rocking it, you badass!

Power Thought

Don't settle for second-best when the best is still out there.

Meet My New Employee, Stephanie ... I Mean Jan

I recently met with a new client and was introduced to their new employee, Stephanie. "But we call her Jan." said my client.

Wait ... what?

Apparently when Stephanie first started her job, my client said to her, "What's up, man?"

She asked, "Did you just call me Jan?"

The name stuck; everyone in the office calls her Jan! When my client told me this story—in front of Stephanie—everyone laughed and laughed, including Stephanie. I now call her Jan as well. The camaraderie in that office means more to the employees than we can really measure, because moments like these are what create company culture. When you have this type of easy rapport with your staff, the harder conversations like those around mistakes are actually easier to have. Business runs smoother and people are more willing to try new things. When people try new things, innovation happens, growth occurs and turnover is reduced. That's why hiring the right candidate, your *ideal* candidate, is so important. The ideal candidate is one who will not only fit into your company culture, but will embrace and nurture it! Remember: A rose by any other name ... would still be Jan. Or Stephanie.

Power Thought

Everyone wants to belong, so be cognizant of creating a welcoming environment.

I met with a client whose business is in a period of rapid growth. His business has grown so fast over the last six months that his brand-new office space (occupied for only a year) is suddenly too small. At the same time, he came across an ideal employee that he just *had* to hire. While he had already renegotiated a deal with his landlord to add more square footage in the near future, he had a big problem for the present: Where was the new employee going to work? Every office was full. The main room had been reconfigured several times and there was no way to squeeze in another desk. Even the conference room had a contract employee using it.

When I asked the client where they ended up locating the new employee, he grinned and said, "We put him at the table in the break room." Sound crazy? Actually, it may have been the best place possible to put a new employee. Usually a new employee's first day consists of filling out paperwork, reading an employee handbook filled with dos and don'ts, parking rules and termination policies, and then the employee is put at a desk with little or no agenda. Other employees are busy trying to complete their own work and they don't normally have the time to approach a new person on their team. While the onboarding process is a necessary one, it is typically not very friendly for the new hire. Locate that same new hire in the break room and the situation takes on an entirely different tone. While people are taking a break, they are generally more relaxed and more social. They have a moment to chat while the coffee maker is brewing; more importantly, they don't need to come up with a reason to seek out and approach the new employee—they're right here!

In this case, the new employee was greeted with enthusiasm every time someone walked in to get a cup of coffee. He was included in "water cooler" talk several times a day, and he was incorporated into the company culture quickly and seamlessly. "This is the best place I have ever worked!" the new employee exclaimed.

If you're looking to break away from the traditional onboarding process while minimizing the time it takes to familiarize new hires with your company's culture, perhaps the break room is the "break" you're looking for!

Power Thought

Sometimes the unconventional is the most conventional.

When Phyllis Francis represented the United States in the 400-meter race, she completed her semi-final looking very relaxed. She won both her first round heat and her semifinal heat easily with a time of 50.58 seconds and 50.31 seconds, respectively. When a reporter asked her what she was thinking about during one of the races, she talked about listening to the advice of her coach who said, "Maintain your form and go for the win."

That concept is deceptively simple, and yet so vitally important in sports—and in hiring as well. Often, clients want to quit the hiring process before we have completed it. They are tired of interviewing and they just want to hire someone ... anyone! The temptation to just stop and say "good enough" is overwhelming. It is the final portion of the race that is the hardest to accomplish, and yet the most important: The last five pounds to lose; the last 10 percent of rehab on an injury; the last few yards to cross the finish line. That last interview with yet another candidate when you are totally frustrated falls into that category. Staying focused on your strategy and following through all the way to the end is the path to victory. Maintain your form, and go for the win. You can do it!

Power Thought
A disciplined mindset keeps you
moving towards your goal.

I recently had multiple conversations with several clients on the topic of leadership skills. The most commonly-held "deep dark secret" of those in a leadership role is that they feel to some degree unprepared or inadequate in the skills needed to lead others. As one client put it, "I'm not much of a leader, Beth; I feel like I am winging it all the time!"

Most people currently in a leadership role didn't start in their industry with the intention of being a leader; they started in their industry in order to do the work within that industry. Along the way, as they gained experience and were promoted, they began directing and coordinating the efforts of others. Their role has changed, and they feel unprepared for the responsibilities, even after several years in the position! What's more, they often feel that asking for assistance is a sign of weakness. Nothing could be further from the truth. No one is skilled at everything, and no one is so good that they can't benefit from improvement. In fact, a leader is in a unique position to establish a culture of improvement for their organization by honestly and gracefully accepting negative feedback.

I recently read a of a true leader's healthy response to such a situation[11]:

> Bob stood up and read his evaluation out loud. It was not pretty. There were lots of problems and weaknesses that his team had identified. He had basically flunked. As the 100 top leaders sat there, listening to Bob read his report, the place was absolutely quiet. Then Bob said, "I'm going to post this outside my office. Then I'll be getting to work on following these recommendations and changing how I lead. In three months, I'll be asking my direct reports to evaluate me again, and I'll also post those results, so you can see my progress.

He continued:

> In these times of change, the only way this organization, and our jobs, have a chance of surviving, is that we need to make some big changes, quickly. You've just seen my personal plan for change. Now I look forward to seeing yours.

---

1   http://www.dailygood.org/story/1365/when-the-boss-flunked-aryae-coopersmith

Then Bob walked out of the room and no one said a word.

Acknowledging shortcomings isn't easy, but it is the only way to honestly address and improve upon them. Leading by example in this way demonstrates that change is necessary, possible and needed for every member of the organization. Do you have the courage to fail? More importantly, do you have the courage to fail like Bob?

Power Thought

Humility is a badge that real leaders are willing to wear.

When I founded A-list Interviews in 2006, one of the first books I read was Martin Yate's *Hiring The Best*, which describes the interviewing process as a "dirty secret" in business, written in 1994. He observed that we promote people within our organizations, ask them to assemble and manage teams, then hold them accountable to the performance of that team without actually giving them the proper skills to be successful. We invest in skills training for goal achievement and leadership, yet rarely do we invest in their ability to conduct effective interviews.

I've had to ask myself, "Why after 20 plus years is this still a dirty secret? Why haven't we had a global conversation about interviewing?" People mistakenly believe that conducting an interview is an easy process that comes naturally. "It is something that we feel we are expected to know, or that comes with experience. Couple that feeling with the average ego and you get 'It's easy enough to interview; I know a good one when I see one; It's sort of a gut feel,'" states Martin Yate.

Sadly, statistics do not support that assertion. According to Peter Drucker, founder of The Drucker Institute[1], two-thirds of all hiring decisions are found to be a mistake within the year. That is a 66 percent failure rate. Here is the bottom line: successfully interviewing candidates is *not* a process based on intuition, instinct, gut feel or judgment. It is a skillset like any other, and it can be taught. How do I know this? Because of MY dirty secret: I made an exceptionally bad hire that made national news. In dealing with the aftermath, I was forced to put my ego aside and admit that even though I thought I knew how to hire effectively, it was obvious that I needed a better process. I launched an enormous research project to figure out how to interview people effectively for the best hire, which became the beginning of A-list Interviews.

---

1   http://www.druckerinstitute.com/peter-druckers-life-and-legacy

Don't continue to carry around your dirty secret. The only way to learn and grow is to admit what you don't know and ask for help. Let me teach you how to interview people, so that you and your company can be hugely successful!

Power Thought

Successful people have a coach to help them improve on their strengths and overcome their weaknesses.

"I'm **FLUENT in** *six* **languages** AND speak *IN 200* different FONTS."

Have you ever seen a bunch of live crabs put into a bowl? They crawl on top of each other, trying to get out, and the crab on top is pulled down by the others. Ultimately, there is so much fighting for the top position that the crabs just wear themselves out. What a crabby bunch!

What do you do when you have your own bunch of crabby employees? Whatever you do, don't crab back at them—doing so is the equivalent of that crab bowl, with everyone stepping on everyone else. In other words, quit complaining! This is the moment when you need to be the leader and help elevate everyone's mood and energy level. Here are a few suggestions:

- *Bring Legos to a staff meeting.* One reason that people get crabby is because they need a distraction. Instead of your ordinary Monday morning staff meeting, do something different to help your employees think outside the bowl.

- *Encourage Volunteering.* There have been many studies that prove getting out of the office improves productivity, creativity and morale. I have a client who has a volunteer policy: A different employee per month chooses their favorite charity, and on the last Friday of the month the whole team goes to volunteer.

- *Re-stating the end goal.* Many candidates talk about how unhappy they are at work. One common reason is because they have lost sight of the company goal and how they fit into that picture. Why are we doing what we are doing? What is my purpose here in this company? How are my efforts contributing to the big picture? As the leader, the more articulate you can be about this, the more satisfied your staff will be.

- *Say Thank You.* I am continually surprised by how effective a simple "thank you" is. At a reunion of my former restaurant workers, I received communication from several former employees, and many of them told me how my thanking them before they left every day had a huge impact on each of them. Several have adopted that habit as leaders.

One final tip: Remember that organizational attitude flows from the top down. If your crabby employees complain all the time, ask yourself if you are complaining all the time. If so, try these tips for yourself!

Power Thought

Imitation is the sincerest form of flattery—good and bad.

"In your employment contract,
you agreed to work for 100k."

Have a problem to solve?
Drive across Kansas.

For various reasons, I have driven across Kansas several times in the last three months. Holy cow, is it boring! Driving east from Colorado on I-70, I soon find yourself with very little to see and even less to do. By the time I get to Hays, Kansas, your entertainment options are limited to the barrage of billboards near the highway or one of the three radio stations within range (two religious and one that plays both kinds of music: country *and* western). I am talked out, tired and sick of listening to crappy radio. Internet connection is iffy at best. There is nothing to see but fields and fields of various grains. I change lanes merely because I need a change of scenery. I contemplate the meaning of "Rock Chalk Jay Hawk." I almost become delirious with boredom ... then something miraculous happens. Just about the time that I think I am going to pull my hair out one strand at a time, I get an idea. I solve a problem that I have been working on forever or I have a flash of insight into a situation I've been frustrated by. I am suddenly inspired about what to do next, and I spend the rest of the trip fleshing out that idea or inspiration. It. Happensb. Every. Time.

In the age of digital media, we don't allow ourselves to get bored. It's too easy to distract ourselves with endless TV shows, multiple social media platforms and an infinite number of ways to play solitaire. But we need to be bored: Out of boredom comes creativity! When we empty our brains of all our obligations, work, home, family, then and only then are our minds free to move creatively.

The next time you have a problem to solve, drive across Kansas. Leave your phone / TV / computer off for an entire day. Stare at corn fields. Think about the meaning of "Rock Chalk Jay Hawk." Think about billboards. Think about nothing. And if you happen to figure out the whole "Rock Chalk Jay Hawk" thing, please explain it to me. Cheers!

Power Thought

In order to innovate,
you have to allow room in your brain. Get bored!

On a road trip across Kansas, I had been driving for hours under blue skies, with temperatures in the 70s and no wind. Suddenly, the only radio station within reception range broke into the broadcast with a tornado warning. Tornado warning? There wasn't a cloud in the sky! What are they talking about? There must be some mistake. Faster than I thought possible, the black clouds rolled in. The rain came down so hard that it was difficult to see the road ahead. The wind picked up dramatically, and off to the right I saw the tornado. Then, as quickly as it started … it was over. Luckily, there was very little damage, but I will never look at Kansas the same way again. The tornado seemed to come out of nowhere, but in retrospect it didn't. I had warnings, I just didn't listen to them.

A similar situation happens to businesses more often than they care to admit. In fact, this is almost exactly what happened to Wells Fargo Bank. The sales quota scandal didn't come out of nowhere. There were multiple warnings to HR, to managers, to the Executive Team … and every warning was ignored. The cost, both monetarily and to their firm's reputation, has been and will continue to be astronomical.

If you hear rumors or whispers of something going on in your business that don't seem right, know that those are usually the tip of the iceberg. It is almost always far bigger than you are aware of, and you must heed those warnings quickly. It is the only way to avoid your business being swept up by a tornado.

Power Thought

Storms in life are inevitable;
heeding the warning signs is the key to survival.

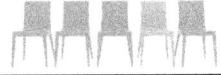

In my early 20s, I worked as a manager in a retail store, and one of my co-workers was a middle-aged woman with three children. After working there for some time, her husband was offered his dream job and the opportunity to move back to California near both of their families. It was a perfect fit for everyone, and my co-worker and her family were beyond ecstatic. Our boss, however, was less than thrilled. Rather than share in her excitement, she was furious at my co-worker for leaving the organization. "How could you possibly leave me now?! I depend on you!" This woman gave my co-worker the silent treatment for the remaining two weeks of her notice.

On her last day, my co-worker hugged me tight and said, "Don't stay here for much longer. This is a toxic place to work."

During that time, I learned one small lesson of what *not* to do as a boss. I made a vow that when my staff turned in their notices, I would handle it differently. I would tell them how happy I was for their new opportunity and I would ask them how I could help them leave on a good note, with the door left open for the future. Most of all, I would thank them for their service to my business.

This commitment to my staff, even as they were leaving my employment, has served me well in countless ways, not the least of which is the fact that allowing someone to exit on a good note feels good to all parties—you, the employee, their co-workers, your clients, etc. Everyone has had a bad boss at some point. Not all bad bosses stay bad bosses. In the case of my former boss, she was under extreme stress at the time, which affected her behavior. In fact, the business ended up closing several years later. Today, she and I are on great terms, and I adore her.

Tell me what lessons you learned from your bad boss; inquiring minds want to know!

Power Thought

Life presents many learning moments, and those who are teachable are lifelong students.

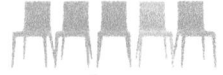

I want to share some success numbers with you. I have a client[1], MEP Engineering, whom I have worked with for some time. They have embraced A-list Interviews process wholeheartedly. In fact, in their latest newsletter, they highlighted their hiring process as one of the reasons their firm has been so successful.

In using A-list Interviews' 7-Step Process, they've been able to efficiently screen an average of 50 candidates for each offer they make. They've achieved a 21 percent growth rate in 2016; the average employee growth rate for their industry is 3.5 percent.[2] In addition, while the average staff turnover rate for their industry is 13.3 percent, their turnover rate was 1 percent.

Figures like that show a rapidly expanding organization whose hiring process that keeps pace with increasing demand and is finely tuned to identify quality candidates. That's what success looks like. Congratulations to MEP Engineering on your tremendous growth! It's been a pleasure working with you. May you continue to be prosperous and successful!

Power Thought

Success is not haphazard, and processes and procedures
are keys to achieving it.

---

1   http://www.mep-eng.com
2   https://www.deltek.com/en/learn/blogs/deltek-vision/2016/06/37th-annual-clarity-architecture-and-engineering-industry-report

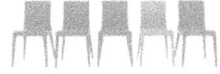

When I begin a new employee search with a client, we start with an exercise to create The Ideal List. It begins with this question: If you dream big about the ideal candidate for this position, who would they be and what would they know? After the list is created, I type it out and send it to the client with instructions to print out the list and post it strategically where they will see and review it regularly. As Napoleon Hill wrote in *Think and Grow Rich*, you can't have what you want unless you know what it is. And you *have* to write it down!

Later, when we meet to continue the process, I ask where they posted their list. Some of the responses I've received are so funny! Here are some of the most memorable:

- *The Coffee Pot.* One of my clients drinks quite a lot of coffee throughout the day, and he has his list posted right behind the coffee pot. He told me, "I know that I will see it there several times a day, morning, noon and night, so it just made sense to me. Also, I had to add to the Ideal List that my perfect employee would also like coffee!"

- *The Washing Machine.* Another client posted her list on top of her washing machine. "I have four kids. I do five loads of laundry per day, so I am definitely going to stare at that list while folding laundry."

- *The Bathroom.* Oddly enough, this is the most common place that people post their list! I've lost count of the number of clients who have told me this. As one client so aptly put it, "It is where I do my best thinking." (Talk about multi-tasking!)

- *The Shower.* I have an amazing client who laminated his list and hung it high in his shower. "I solve the world's problems when I am in the shower. I look up while I am washing/rinsing my hair, and I stare at that list."

Where would you post your Ideal List? I would love to hear!

Power Thought

Out-of-the-box thinking leads to out-of-the-box solutions.

"Allen is an incredibly wonderful, generous, exciting, fun, kind, loving, brilliant, very special human being. This personal reference from your dog is quite impressive."

Three Ways That Writing a
Book Is Like Interviewing

Many authors have described writing as a lengthy and arduous process. I had been in the process of writing my first book *Why Can't I Hire Good People? Lessons on How to Hire Better* for several years, and it seemed I had been doing so forever! However, after I put the final touches on my manuscript sent to the publisher, I was struck by how amazing this process has been (even though there were times when I wanted to pull my hair out). The learning, the soul searching, the patience and persistence have all been incredible lessons. As I write, rewrite, delete, and continue to revise my vision, I realize the process of writing a book is much like the process of interviewing for new employees: The book that I thought I was writing when I began this process is not the book that I ended up writing. I envisioned the process of writing a book was similar to the process of reading one—you start at the beginning and write steadily and smoothly until you've reached the end. I was unprepared for the number of revisions, edits, rewrites and rearranging that occurs ... and the same thing happens in the process of interviewing candidates for a position.

My clients are surprised that midway through the process, we may change the job title, change the scope of the position or change the current department structure because we have a better idea of what we need. You truly do not know what you are looking for until you begin the search, any more than I knew what book I would be writing until I started to write it.

Never, never, never give up! Those wise words were uttered by the amazing Winston Churchill. There were so many times that I wanted to just quit writing. I got stuck, had writer's block, or just became fed up with the whole process and would exclaim, "That's it! I give up!" About that time, I would have a breakthrough that gave my book and my vision for it new energy.

When you are interviewing for new employees, you will have bad days. You will think, "I am *never* going to find someone!" Then suddenly, because you kept at it, a person walks in and restores your faith, both in the new employee and in your business. You realize that all of your struggles have been worth it. Much like completing a book, when you have finished the search, when you have found your Ideal Person and you have completed the hiring process, you feel like you could "leap tall buildings in a single bound!" You forget the times when you got stuck, frustrated, impatient, and the times where you hated the process. Instead, you feel like you won the lottery! While you continue the search for A-list employees—just like me completing the final phase of publishing my book—remember this: Anything worth having is worth the trouble of making it happen, whether writing a book or hiring your next superstar.

Power Thought

Anything worth finishing is worth finishing the right way.

How the Unemployment Rate Affects Your Recruiting

As of this writing, Colorado has the lowest unemployment rate in over 40 years. This is very good news! Having the majority of people employed something to celebrate. However, it can make for a very long recruiting process. If you are hiring, this is the time that you can make fear-based mistakes, so here are four tips to keep you calm and focused while you are searching for your amazing hire.

1. *Create your Ideal List and stick to it.* Regardless of the unemployment rate, employers needing to fill a position feel the pressure of urgency—hurry up already and just find someone! But rushing a hiring decision rarely, if ever, results in a good hire. Envision the employee you really want and stick to your vision, even when you feel that pressure.

2. *Read over your Ideal List.* Get excited over how much better things will be when you find your great hire, and then read your Ideal List again!

3. *Get creative and thorough with your outreach.* You never know where your great hire will be found, so make sure you're looking everywhere you can. Utilize the network of people you know: talk to your neighbors, your friends, your children's friends' parents ... everyone. Also, make sure that your message appears everywhere online, not only in the networks you frequent. For instance, people who regularly use Facebook might post their message there, but they'll never reach the ideal candidate who doesn't log on to Facebook but who regularly uses Indeed.com. Your outreach should be as large as possible, and may include some unconventional methods: I talked to one employer who leaves her business card with people that she thinks will be good hires.

4. *Check your brand online.* Jobseekers will research you and your company, and if they see negative information they will be less likely to apply. When is the last time you've done a Google search on your company, or checked what Glassdoor and Amazon say about your company? Make sure you know what potential candidates are seeing about you.

In a market with low unemployment, finding your ideal candidate may take longer than under different circumstances. However, keep in mind that even under the best of circumstances, finding your ideal candidate will seem like it takes forever! It can be a stressful situation. Be comforted in knowing that every other company is in the same boat; let them be the ones who buckle under the fear and stress and make impulsive and costly hiring mistakes. Stay calm, stay focused and hang in there!

Power Thought

Having confidence in yourself and
your processes will allow you to wait patiently.

---

1   http://www.bizjournals.com/denver/news/2017/06/05/unemployment-colorado-cities-counties-are-the.html

Three Full-Time and Two Part-Time Boyfriends

When my daughter Katy was 17, she was sitting around with her two BFFs when one girl asked, "Katy, how many boyfriends do you have?"

The other girl jumped in and said, "I know! She has three full-time and two part-time boyfriends!"

When the first girl looked puzzled, Katy replied, "Well, I get different things from each of them." She explained that boyfriend #1 provides freedom and challenges her intellectually, boyfriend #2 brings flowers and is fiercely loyal, and boyfriend #3 is the perfect group date, as his best friends are dating Katy's best friends. As for the two part-time boyfriends, #1 provides companionship and reliability, while #2 is convenient as she sees him every day.

Katy has always been encouraged to not settle for someone who doesn't meet all of her criteria. She shouldn't settle, because she deserves the best of the best.

In hiring, we often see similar situations with candidates. One will possess the experience the employer feels is vital, another will be a proven team player, yet another exudes enthusiasm. Just this past week, one of my clients exclaimed, "Beth, if we could just combine these two candidates, we'd have the perfect employee!" Since combining two people into one is only possible in science fiction (and those stories almost always end up badly), many people in this position will try to convince themselves to hire Candidate A because he or she is a better fit than any of the other candidates. This path almost always ends up badly as well, except the result isn't fiction: It's your business reality. If you are in this situation, the better plan of action is to re-read your vision for the ideal candidate, redouble your efforts and hold out for the right fit! Remember the advice to Katy: "You shouldn't settle, because you deserve the best of the best."

Power Thought

Bottom line: Don't settle.

I interviewed a woman who had previously been an office manager for a thriving company. She understood that her job was one with wide-ranging responsibilities that required many and various tasks. When I asked what prompted her to resign, she replied, "When I had to sell the owners' roosters on Craigslist."

Had this woman's job been at a farm working with animals, this request might not have seemed so egregious. However, she was working in an office setting with many other employees, so a request like this was quite a bit outside the normal boundaries of the job and she felt taken advantage of.

This is just one example of the importance of having an accurate job description for every position. The job description helps the employee know what is expected of them, and gives them guidelines on how to be successful in the role. When an employee is asked to do something far outside the boundaries of the job, they can feel uncomfortable, uneasy and unsure on how to proceed. This is not the way to build a productive and satisfying relationship with an employee.

I know, I know ... writing a job description is boring, boring, boring! My clients tell me this regularly, and it is usually coupled with an eye roll. However, having a document that accurately describes the job can benefit both the employer and the prospective employee by laying out the tasks, responsibilities and expectations beforehand, in black and white. If you don't own a farm and aren't in the animal husbandry industry, don't ask your employee to sell your roosters (unless you write it in the job description!) Then when the rooster crows, everyone knows what to expect. Cock-a-doodle-doo!

Power Thought

Feeling valued and appreciated—and not taken advantage of—is key to loyalty and commitment.

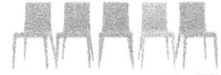

When my daughter Katy had her homecoming as a junior in high school, she was also a cheerleader, and somehow became responsible for doing everyone's hair on the squad before the game. Katy's role as squad hairdresser started as a sophomore, when she created a beautiful, complicated braid for her own hair. All of the other girls wanted that hair style as well. Katy googled hairstyles, watched YouTube videos, and practiced on her hair (and everyone else's) in order to be promoted to Head Hair Stylist for the Cardinal Cheer Squad.

I asked her, "What are they going to do when you graduate?!"

She shot back, "Oh, I am training Jordan to do this job when I graduate."

Of course she is. This process of having people hire and train their own replacement when they advance is exactly how successful companies grow, develop their staff and how innovation occurs. Those people who are on the front lines do research, they learn, they improve the company's processes and they teach the next generation to do the same. I would imagine that the Cardinal Cheer Squad will have the best hairstyles for years to come, thanks to Katy!

When you have an employee who wants to learn something new and take on a new task, let them. After all ... hair today. Gone tomorrow.

Power Thought

Training goes a long way to ensuring consistency
in your business.

Don't Use This F-Word to Describe Your Work Environment

There are plenty of great words that start with the letter F that you might use to describe the people you work with and the culture within your organization. Words come to mind such as Fun, Fantastic, Fabulous, Fulfilling, Fast, Fundamental, Fantabulous, Functioning, Fitting, Fashionable, Friendly, Fortunate, Famous, Fortuitous...just to name a few. But there is one F-word that you should *never* use to describe your work environment: Family. That's right, never ever use the word "family" to describe the people you work with.

A family is a group of people closely related by blood, and you can't do anything about that. You can't fire your cousin from being your cousin, if he or she constantly makes poor choices and avoidable mistakes. However, you can—and should!—fire anyone who works for you who does that. I hear this all the time: "He told me that we were family, and then he fired me!" "Family doesn't fire you." "She lied. We weren't family. If we were, I wouldn't have gotten fired."

If you are searching for a word that describes your company culture, try some of these: Tribe, Troupe, Village, Community, Group, Team ... but don't confuse your employees by using the term family.

Power Thought

Replace the family tree with an organizational chart!

Most of my clients would tell you that I have seen everything there is to see when it comes to interviewing candidates. I will tell you this just isn't true. People in general continue to surprise me, even more so during the interview process.

I recently encountered a "first" when interviewing a candidate. While conducting a phone interview with an applicant for a high-level position, his dog barked consistently in the background. Attempting to keep the dog quiet, the gentleman used a squeaky toy to try to distract the dog, which of course, only excited the dog more. Squeak! Squeak! Bark! Bark! "I am definitely the best fit for this role!" he yelled over the barking dog.

I am all about having dogs. I love them and support companies that allow employees to bring their dogs to work. Studies have shown that dogs help de-stress their owners and I am always an advocate for a less stressful workplace. I also believe in taking excellent care of our beloved pets by providing all the squeaky toys they can handle. Do I believe that dogs belong in an interview for employment? No, I do not.

An interview is a first impression. We are evaluating a candidate's ability to focus, to think on their feet and to listen to the questions asked. If they are busy playing with their dog during an interview, they are telling their potential employer that they are less concerned about him or her and more concerned with their four-legged friend. It may also be a sign they will become distracted easily. If this occurs during one of your interviews for an A-list employee, I recommend a hard pass. Woof!

Power Thought

To stay focused means you have to eliminate distractions ...
even those you may enjoy.

Jeremy is a designer for Calvin Klein. He has worked for his manager, Suzanne, for many years in multiple positions and capacities. They have a fantastic working relationship and have for a long time. Earlier this year, Jeremy' sister was diagnosed with a rare form of liver cancer and was given six months-to-a year to live. Jeremy and his sister have always been very close, so this was devastating news. For the next several months, Jeremy traveled as often as possible from New York to Texas to spend as much time with his sister as possible, then flying back to go work. As his sister grew worse, death was imminent.

One day, Suzanne called Jeremy into her office and said, "I want you to buy a one-way ticket to Texas. Don't come back until this is over. You need to be with your family right now."

Jeremy spent several weeks with his sister before she passed away. He said, "[Suzanne] gave me a gift that I can never re-pay."

I wanted to highlight a story that shows managers and employees can be loyal and supportive of each other. We can treat each other as human beings and love each other through the hardest times of our lives. It is called the human experience. This story exemplifies when the work environment and culture are at their finest. For all the great managers and employees out there, keep up the good work. And Suzanne, you are the epitome of the greatest managers ever. Nice work!

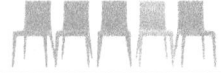

Power Thought

The golden rule, "Treat others as you want to be treated."
is always in vogue.

Right before the holidays, I had a potential client call me frustrated with an employee. "I just gave out bonuses, and she wants more money ... I don't know what to do!" Having seemingly entitled employees is a hot topic of conversation these days. Here are my thoughts: An entitled employee is in the wrong job.

Think about it. When an employee is in a job they love, they are happy. They think about the work that they "get to do," not what they "have to do." They may ask for a raise or for more vacation time, but rarely are these on the forefront of their minds. They are excited to work every day because they are passionate about their objectives. They feel confident and are thriving.

But when they are not happy in their jobs? They will do anything to keep themselves engaged. They think that money will make them happy. They think that more time off will make them happy. Or free movie tickets, a gift certificate for a massage or getting to work from home. But in the end, if they are not enjoying their jobs anymore, have a conversation with these employees about doing something else or let them go. Nothing can make up for doing work that they do not enjoy, and I do mean nothing! When you have an entitled employee, don't talk about more money, benefits, working from home, etc.; it won't help, and only increases frustration for both you and your employee. Instead, talk about the job duties, and ask if this is really the work they love. If it's not? Either move them to a position that is right for them, or help them transition out gracefully. Always remember, you as the employer are entitled to an employee who wants to do the job you are offering.

Power Thought

Gratitude and ungratefulness
will breed polar opposite people.

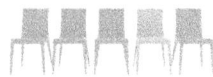

I ate lunch with a client at an adorable café in Denver, CO. They had listed on the menu a kale and quinoa salad that included "Market Finds."

I asked the kind server, "What is a 'Market Find'?"

She smiled widely and replied, "We go to the market every day to buy our ingredients. A "Market Find" is whatever we find that looks good at the market that day."

That day the market find was golden beets ... yum!

Her statement suddenly struck me as relevant to interviewing for employees. I teach my clients about the importance of an ideal candidate description, and yet this server reminded me that we can sometimes be too rigid with our expectations. When we are hiring for a new employee, we can make the requirements so strict that we miss what is amazing about a person and their potential contributions to our teams. Common examples that I hear for firm requirements often relate to experience levels and skill sets. There are some jobs where specific certifications, education and/or skill level are required, but often employers get hung up on a candidate having a skill set that can be easily taught.

Yes, I am an advocate for having a baseline to measure for a great candidate. Be sure to also leave room for "Market Finds" that open the door to out-of-the-box candidates. These hidden treasures can often be what life is all about, and you can't "beet" that.

Power Thought

Firm expectations that allow for flexibility will often lead
to the unexpected gifts life has to offer.

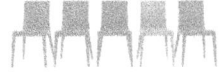

One particular week, I made four job offers, which is rather unusual for me. After the third interview, once we have selected *the* candidate, I call their references. Reference calls are a big debate in my industry. Should you? Shouldn't you? As one client so eloquently stated, "Why do I want to call a bunch of people who love this person?" Here is why: Because they love this person.

I made 12 reference calls in two days. As a result, my faith in humanity and my ability to interview and hire great people was reinforced. Some of the comments I heard about the four candidates about to receive a job offer were: "I know that you will love working with him as much as I did." "You are so lucky to have her!" "He is welcome back here anytime." "What a great guy. If I could hire him away from you, I would."

Reference calls are specifically designed to get a feel for someone outside of the interview process to give you additional insight into the person you are about to hire. The information that you get can aid in your assessment of a person's work ethic, likeability, cultural fit and integrity. Good references are eager to help their friend/co-worker/employee get to the next phase of their career. Their words speak volumes and are a telling sign of a great new employee when their references call back quickly. Get at least three references from your potential new hires. Ask for managers and co-workers, and tailor your questions to that particular candidate. Then, pick up the phone and call those references. If you feel like I did yesterday, you can make the job offer with confidence. Happy, happy hiring!

Power Thought
One's reputation is reinforced by the words of others.

I am learning how to box. Unbeknownst to me, much of the work in boxing is through your legs. You must be able to avoid the competitor's swing by moving around. "Float like a butterfly; sting like a bee," said Mohammed Ali. And he was right!

To the observer, boxing looks like punching is the top priority, it isn't. The boxer wins, not through the jab but by not running out of steam in his or her legs. My instructor tells me that the secret to not running out of steam in your legs is to recruit the hamstrings to do their part. They are the largest muscle in the body so making your quads do all the work is inefficient. You must invite the hamstrings to engage, to participate, and to do the heavy lifting. Do you know how *hard* this is? I am so used to letting the front of my legs carry the load that I don't have any idea how to recruit my hamstrings! Ugh.

The word "recruit" inspired me to think about how we engage our employees. We all have those few people who carry the weight of the team, and we let them. It is easier in the short-term to rely on those that you have relied on before. But, as my boxing instructor says, "This is bad mechanics." When you rely too heavily on one small group (of employees or muscles), you end up burning them out. This is how we end up with injured muscles or people who quit. You have to recruit others on your team to take on new challenges in order to be a well-rounded, balanced organization. Encourage cross-training and sharing of ideas that create efficiencies. Maybe the quiet one in a meeting has the idea that will carry the business forward in entirely new ways! You won't know until you ask. When assigning tasks and duties on your team, remember to mix it up. Have people lead the way who don't normally take on leadership responsibilities. Ask someone who never volunteers to complete a special task. When you recruit the large muscles to do the heavy lifting, you are a better leader. And boxer. Here's to your health and success!

Power Thought

Encourage. Inspire. Challenge.
These three words are game-changers!

My daughter Katy was just selected to participate in a Chem-a-thon, a chemistry marathon through her high school. It is a very high honor ... sort of. For those students who are selected, they "get" to drive on a bus for 1 ½ hours to go take a four-hour standardized test, then drive back to school for another 1 ½ hours in the middle of the hardest year, and the most challenging time of year in high school. In addition, they are still held accountable for other tests, papers and group projects that are due before the end of the year. As Katy so eloquently put it, "You want to be chosen. You just don't want to *do* it. And I even have to *buy* my own t-shirt!" Is this reward really a reward?

While I was at a client's office, I overheard some employees complaining about being "rewarded" for being chosen to sit on an advisory committee for their manager. Same thing. They wanted to be chosen, but there were so many extra projects that were required, with no extra time to complete them and no extra resources to get the projects completed. One employee sighed, "Working all weekend is *not* a reward!"

Rewarding your employees can be so satisfying for both parties. It can dramatically improve morale and it is a great way to create a culture that all parties love. Just make sure that the reward is actually a reward. And, please, please, *please* don't make them buy their own t-shirts!

Power Thought
A reward is only a reward, if it truly rewards.

My daughter Katy starts cheerleading practice soon. As the lead cheerleader, she wants to wear a great outfit on the first day. She looked high and low for her favorite pair of cheer shorts, but to no avail. Bitterly disappointed, she bought another pair, but still, she wanted to find her favorites. Then, it struck her. They might be in the trunk of her car. "My trunk is the new junk drawer," she exclaimed! "I throw everything back there."

Sure enough, after searching her trunk, there were her beloved shorts along with two blankets, a shirt that she had also "lost," a curling iron, a pair of shoes, and some Valentine's Day wrapping paper that she doesn't remember buying. Katy took a few hours to get everything back to where it was supposed to be, and life appears to have calmed for my teenage daughter. Does Katy's struggle sound familiar?

Often, we spend an immense amount of time looking for things we already have, only to repurchase and rediscover the item along with a series of other things you had forgotten about. The same can be true for your office, talent pool and business processes. You know when it is time to clean up when *every* little task takes way more time than it should. You look for a document but can't easily find it due to an unorganized filing system. You look for a colleague's phone number, but it was not entered into your contact database. All these little tasks end up taking an inordinate amount of time—time that could be spent on business activities.

I encourage you to "shake out the rugs" in your business departments, clean up job descriptions, re-organize the filing cabinets, create new habits to prevent the loss of information and start with a new, ruthlessly organized ... trunk. You will be glad that you did!

Power Thought

Cleaning and organization will give you something
everyone desires: control.

Is Your Bad Employee Holding You Back?

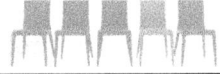

I received a call last week from a woman I had never met. She was an employer who wanted to ask me some questions about firing an employee who is "making my life a living hell." I asked her to explain why she believed the person was an underperforming employee. She replied, "She is doing nothing towards her job and everything to make everyone else's job harder."

"Can you give me an example?" I asked.

"I sure can. She called a long-term vendor of mine and cancelled an order that we had placed. This order was instrumental in getting a project done for our top client. Luckily, I have a fantastic relationship with this vendor, who called me personally to make sure the order should be cancelled. This is not the first time, nor is it the first incident. In addition, she shows up late, none of her work is done on time, and her attitude is turning away new clients."

"How long has this been going on?" I asked.

"Five years."

I gasped. Why on earth did this woman put up with an unacceptable employee for as long as she did? There are a few reasons an employer will keep a poor employee in place:

- The employee was not performing unsatisfactorily for the whole five years, just part of it. The employer creates a false sense of "it will get better over time."

- You have a conversation with an underperforming employee and it gets better for a short time. Then a new erosion of performance begins. The employer begins to believe this is just a cycle of behavior to justify.

- The employer thinks they cannot have an empty position while they hire someone else. Since many do not like the hiring process, they delay the search.

- They feel bad for firing someone.

191

Here is what I told her: "I greatly appreciate that you want to provide a good working environment for your employees, and I understand that you feel bad. In the 16 years I have been doing this, I have never had a client tell me that they regretted firing an employee. Not one. I have had clients regret hiring someone and regret not firing them sooner, but I have never had a client regret firing an employee."

If it has crossed your mind that you need to fire an employee, begin to truly examine the situation. If you determine the employee is no longer a fit, follow a consistent firing policy, including documentation and explaining the severity of your dissatisfaction to the employee. And, don't wait. You are just putting off the inevitable. As they say in business, hire slow, fire fast.

Power Thought

Delaying the inevitable will only prolong the inevitable.

My daughter Katy had exactly one week left to finish her junior year of high school. As you can well imagine, she was in a mad panic about how she was going to get everything done. She had four papers due that week, six tests, two group projects, teacher gifts, cheerleading obligations as the head cheerleader for next year, graduation gifts for her friends and she promised to make cupcakes for her friend's graduation party. For someone who is ultra-organized and always has a to-do list a mile long, this was still a ton of work to be done!

Completely overwhelmed with the number of things to do, one night she just completely lost it and started crying, worried that she wouldn't get everything done in time. Once she got it out of her system, she rallied, and finished the work that she needed to get done.

What happens when this occurs to your staff at work? Here are some things that you can do to help your staff get through a stressful time of year, and/or a huge project that must be completed:

- In the moment, remind your staff that this is short term, and it won't last forever.

- Have very clear expectations about what needs to be accomplished.

- Help your staff prioritize their duties, so that they know how to get the work done.

- Make a plan to celebrate when this period is complete: have a party, give your people an extra day off or plan an outing of some kind.

- Encourage exercise, breaks and healthy eating.

- Have snacks. "We never meet unless we eat!" is a great mantra in general.

- Take a group walk over the lunch hour.

- And finally, show your gratitude for their dedication. Say thank you. Often.

Katy ended her school year with grace, style and outstanding grades. I couldn't be more proud of her! We all get overwhelmed. We can only hope to have as much grace and fortitude as my beautiful teenager.

Power Thought

When overwhelmed, take a deep breath and remind yourself, "This too shall pass."

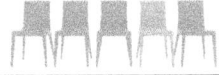

For those of you who know me well, you know that I am a total nerd when it comes to interviewing. I read everything I can get my hands on about this particular topic. As an expert in the interview process for hiring employees, I was particularly struck by this Fast Company article titled *What if we killed the job interview?*[1]" According to the author, organizations make better hiring decisions when they use artificial intelligence (AI) based tools as opposed to actual interviews, so he advocates rather strongly that we ditch interviews altogether. His main point is that hiring managers and recruiters "overestimate their ability 'to interview and evaluate a potential candidates' suitability for the job.'" In other words, their ego gets the better of them.

I agree with him completely that the ego can play a detrimental role when interviewing for new hires. In 1994, Martin Yate wrote in his book, *Hiring The Best*, "[Interviewing] is something that we feel we are expected to know, or that comes with experience.[2] Couple that feeling with the average ego, and you get, 'It's easy enough to interview; I know a good one when I see one; it's sort of a gut feeling.'"

However, the numbers prove otherwise. Two-thirds of all hires are found to be a mistake within the year. Does that mean we should completely stop job interviews? Not in my opinion.

The author in the Fast Company article continues, "Interviews are more useful when they are totally structured and standardized."

1   https://www.fastcompany.com/40579524/what-if-we-killed-the-job-interview
2   https://www.getabstract.com/en/summary/human-resources/hiring-the-best/5459

Exactly. Yet why don't we do this? Structured and standardized interviews provide better data. Most employers will tell you it is because, before now, no one has ever created a structured interview process that works. I have interviewed almost 20,000 candidates using a structured interview system that I needed to create myself and with great success. Intrigued? The whole system is spelled out in my book Why Can't I Hire Good People? available on Amazon.1 Killing the job interview is a terrible suggestion. Improving the structure of the hiring/ interview process makes way more sense.

Power Thought

Improved processes and structure give you confidence in
what you are doing.

1   https://www.amazon.com/Why-Cant-Hire-Good-People/dp/1941870902

© Glasbergen/ glasbergen.com

GLASBERGEN

"I'd like to start out as CEO, then settle into a lower position after my student loans are paid off."

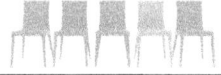

As you know, I've been learning how to box. When I am sparring, I am notorious for dropping my left hand, which means my face is unprotected. My trainer keeps telling me that I am going to get punched in the face if I don't protect myself with the left hand. Do I listen? Eh ... sort of.

This did remind me of a quote from Mike Tyson, the former heavyweight professional boxer, "Everyone has a plan until they get punched in the mouth." I realized my current plan was to land a punch, not protect myself. To really protect my face, I would have to learn how to punch differently. I would have to change the way I do things. It is so easy not to change methods when life and work are going okay. You skate along for a while following a plan, then status quo sets in. You think about ways to improve or make things better without much action. Then, wham! You get punched in the face. Now you want to change and change fast.

I have a client who hired a woman who had worked for him for years. She was mean to clients, obstinate with her boss, and a stickler for doing things *her* way. When a handful of great employees met with my client and told him that they were all leaving because of this woman, he knew he had to do something fast. He had let his left hand drop by keeping her for so long and he got punched in the face with the threat of losing better performing employees. He immediately fired the employee who was difficult and workplace morale dramatically improved.

What took him so long? Change normally requires an impetus. Significant "pain" must be present for the motivation to kick in to make changes, especially when they are perceived as tough to accomplish or hurtful to others. I say punch bad hiring and firing techniques in the mouth and change your processes. Hire and retain great employees and replace those who are not a fit. With A-list Interviews training program, you will improve your plan and learn how to protect your assets. Don't wait.

Power Thought

Change only occurs when the "pain" outweighs the "gain"
of the current circumstances.

Want to Change Your Company Culture? Try Flood Prevention.

One Friday the 13th, I had a meeting planned with one of my favorite clients. I arrived excited to be there and was greeted by the team having a company lunch. I asked my client, "What is the occasion?"

He replied, "Flood prevention."

Oh … Wait! What? Everyone on to the team laughed as they began to fill me in on the joke. Apparently, the company has a cultural tradition of having lunch on Friday the 13th. The one time the company did not have a lunch on this notoriously superstitious date, their conference room flooded. So now, they never miss having a company lunch this day … flood prevention!

During lunch, there was a lot of good-natured ribbing of one another with a very comfortable banter where everyone was included. It was a lighthearted meal that showed how much of a team this group had become. And, I might add, highly productive and efficient. Very often, leadership refers to the people who make up the workforce within the company as "human capital." This reference has always struck me as an odd way to refer to the people, not just "humans," who sell and produce, care for clients and are essentially the lifeblood of a company. They are so much more than "capital," they are essential. This CEO is an excellent example of how our workforce should be referenced. He greets his employees by name, asks about their family members and supports whatever fun his people may be having. He never refers to his staff as "human capital" or "current head count." Instead, he uses words like "team," "crew" and "associates"—much higher titles of respect and acknowledgement.

If you want to change your company culture, begin with your language. Refer to your staff by name, not as "human capital." Then celebrate the people who create success with the occasional company lunch … even if only to ward off superstition. Remember to laugh a lot and chime in on friendly banter. And if you happen to prevent your building from flooding, then congrats … two birds, one stone.

Power Thought

"Flood" your employees with the opportunity to learn, grow and hang out.

Everyone Thinks They Can Make Love, Interview and Drive

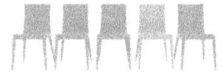

A few years ago, I was speaking about hiring to a group of CPAs. We were discussing the differences between hiring and interviewing, when all of the sudden, a gentleman stood up in the back and shouted, "You know, everyone thinks they can make love, interview and drive." You could have heard a pin drop. Then, someone giggled, and it was all over after that. Still, the question remained for me unanswered: What is it about interviewing for employees that makes people think they can do it without having been taught?

When I mention that I am an interviewer, someone will invariably say to me, "I am a great interviewer."

"How did you learn to be a good interviewer?" I ask.

"Oh, I am a great people person," is a typical response.

I wonder what being a people person has to do with interviewing, which is a skill set that is developed over time. It is not genetic. You aren't born into the world knowing how to interview. It requires education, a process and practice. Yet, the hiring interview—the interaction between a candidate and a potential employer—is the one area in the selection process on which we spend the least amount of time, money and preparation. We don't train our hiring managers or our HR staff on how to conduct an effective interview. It is expected to be inherent knowledge. As Martin Yate said in his book *Hiring the Best*, "...[interviewing] is a dirty secret for many, and a sad comment on old-style management practices that managers are not taught [how to interview]. It is something we feel we are expected to know, or that comes with experience. Couple that feeling with the average ego, and you get 'It's easy enough to interview; I know a good one when I see one; it's sort of a gut feel.'"

With two-thirds of all hiring decisions found to be a mistake within one year, are you sure that you want your ego to lead the way? It is okay not to know. It is okay to ask for help. Call me today: I have a process and the experience needed to arm you with the skills required to interview (and hire) with confidence and results.

Power Thought

Asking for help is a sign of strength, humility and
an open-minded person.

"I have plenty of management experience. I spent
18 years telling my parents what to do."

I received a call from a former client recently who is losing a valued employee. She said, "You know, we weren't using your process back then, and this employee would never have gotten past the third interview."

"Do you know why?" I asked.

She said, "Yes, the third interview is all about passion for a position and this employee doesn't love what we do."

I have had so many hiring managers and CEOs want to shorten the interview process and rob themselves of one of the most critical steps in the hiring process. I completely understand why. Many of them are in a hurry and impatient to fill a position. Some are afraid that they will lose the candidate to another opportunity or worse, they are afraid they will *never* find anyone and just hire someone already! All of this is a perfect recipe to a bad hire. As Warren Buffet so aptly stated, "Money flows from the impatient to the patient." So do candidates, houses, opportunities, etc.

The third interview measures how passionate the candidate is for the work you are offering. If they aren't loving the job you offer, their skillset doesn't matter, their availability doesn't matter and their experience doesn't matter.

Another client called me today and said, "Thank God for the third interview! I just avoided a horrible hiring mistake because I followed the process completely! Thank you, Beth!"

You're welcome! Keep following your interviewing system; it is designed to find you great employees, not "good enough" employees.

Power Thought

Always remember, "Good" is the enemy of "great."

I spoke at a conference in San Antonio for the Independent Bankers Association of the State of Texas (IBAT). I also had the privilege of hearing the CEO, Chris Williston, speak about his 35 years of involvement with the organization as he prepared to exit. He had grown the IBAT into the largest association of independent bankers in the country. It was obvious that he had made great friends in the group and would completely be missed as a leader. His exact quote was, "I have never worked a day in my life." He then shared how grateful he was for the organization, that he loved the people and the work, and that he wished for all people to have the happiness in their jobs like he did. He was passionate, articulate and humble.

I have thought about that speech on and off, and I've realized how rare it is that people feel this way about their job. Why is this so? How is it that Chris, who had "fallen into this job," was so successful? Here are a few observations to Chris' satisfaction:

- There were enough parts of his job that suited him perfectly. He was a natural relationship builder and spent a great deal of his time doing just that: getting to know independent bankers.

- He had enough control in his job that when his constituents needed something done, and it was right for the organization, Chris had the power to get it done.

- Chris had the resources to delegate the work that he disliked to someone else. He could focus on the parts that he loved and passed off the rest.

- He oversaw his own growth and that of the association.

I have so much respect for someone who leaves an organization way better than they found it. Chris Williston is one of those people. Do you empower people in your organization to thrive, contribute and grow? It could be the difference between an unhappy workforce and a happy one.

Power Thought
Whatever you do should contribute to something bigger than yourself.

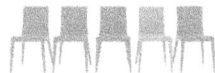

I had a call from a client whom I worked with years ago. We had successfully hired an employee for a very key position in his company. He has called me regularly to share how great of an employee she had become over years. She has been great with his clients, great with her budget, great with the other folks on the team ... He could not have been happier.

Then one day he called to tell me that his "amazing employee" was suddenly dropping the ball. "Beth, I don't understand it! She is making mistakes on things where in the past she has performed flawlessly! I am actually thinking about firing her because it is so bad."

I always advise my clients to first take a big, deep breath when becoming frustrated. Then I advise them to take another big, deep breath and look at performance issues from various perspectives before firing once high-performing employees. I continued the conversation by asking, "Have you asked her what is going on?"

"Well, no. I haven't."

I encouraged my client to talk to his beloved employee with empathy and compassion to uncover what may be behind her sudden shift in behavior. I suggested he state something like this, "You know, I have noticed that you haven't been yourself lately. Are you okay?" As it turns out, she did have some personal trauma happening in her life, discovering someone close to her had been diagnosed with terminal cancer. She confessed to feeling like a total wreck. She also expressed that having a conversation with her manager, my client, was really helpful. While she continued to have a tough go of it for the next several months, she was able to get help when she needed and turn her performance around.

When you see job performance decline in a great employee, before you discipline in any way, check in with their emotional well-being. As a great leader, you will really be glad that you did.

Power Thought

Our emotional well-being affects every part of our lives ... even if we don't realize it. Check in with your people regularly.

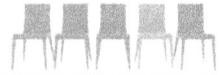

I regularly speak to groups of CEOs who are primarily concerned about hiring. Invariably, someone will tell me that they can't find the right people because the unemployment rate is so low. They talk about how there are "no good employees" out there and because they don't have good employees, they can't expand the way they want. Do you see the slippery slope they just went down?

Irrational thinking as described above is way more impactful on our hiring processes than unemployment rates, regardless of how low they may go. Here are some tips to get you out of the trap of thinking no good employees are available for hire:

- *Create a great place to work.* An article by Bloomberg News[1], people are leaving their jobs at a 17-year high. People are leaving jobs like they did right after 9/11, meaning they are looking for a place to work where their work matters. They want to contribute to something bigger than themselves. Simply put, this is the perfect opportunity to sit down with your direct reports and have a vision conversation about the culture of the company and their roles within it. Ask them where they want to be, what they want to do and how they want to contribute. Then, make it happen for them.

- *Focus on retention.* According to hr.com, employees are four times more likely to be looking for a job if they work for a jerk. So, don't be a jerk. And, don't let your managers be jerks either. If you want good employees to leave your company, keep a jerk on your payroll.

- *Have no fear.* Don't focus on the bad stuff. If you fear that you won't find good employees, you won't. Remember to write your Ideal Candidate List for your best employee and read over it every day. Don't settle. They *are* out there, probably just as frustrated as you are in trying to find you. Which leads me to my last tip....

---

1   https://www.bloomberg.com/news/articles/2018-09-11/job-openings-in-u-s-increased-in-july-to-record-6-94-million

2   https://www.hrdive.com/news/workers-unhappy-with-managers-4x-more-likely-to-job-hunt/542515

- *Create a candidate-friendly interview process.* What does this mean? It means, interview fast. Call the candidates quickly, get them scheduled soon, and make an efficient interview process. Have your basic screening processes in place but do not be ridiculous in your requirements for applying. Then, give the candidates a clear deadline as to when they will have answers, and stick to that deadline. Say no politely, but firmly, and don't leave people hanging. Candidates have lots of choices these days. Be a place that they want to be.

Warren Buffet says that money flows from the impatient to the patient. I say that the same thing happens with candidates: be patient, be thorough and be polite. Happy Hiring!

Power Thought

One of my clients has a list of company values on his wall, and the first one is "Don't be an a$*hole, and don't hire a$*holes." Couldn't have said it better myself.

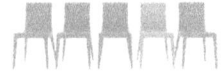

I received a call last week from a potential client who said, "I need help recruiting. Do you do that?"

I told him that I did provide recruiting services, then I asked him, "What makes you think that you need help recruiting?"

He said, "I can't find the right people."

"Have you posted a job advertisement online?"

Yes, he had.

I asked, "Are you getting applicants?" Yes, he was getting applicants. "Then you do not need help recruiting," I told him. "You need help interviewing."

Most business leaders are confused about what recruiting does for their hiring process and what it does not do. *Recruiting* is asking people to apply for a job. *Interviewing* is the screening process to finding someone to work for you. *Hiring* is the yes or no question that you ask yourself before making a job offer.

Recruiting is simply getting the applicants. That's it. No more. No less. So let us be clear on what recruiting does *not* do:

- Recruiting doesn't help you select the right candidate. Interviewing does that.

- Recruiting doesn't help you figure out what you want. Creating an Ideal Candidate Profile and accurate job description does that.

- Recruiting doesn't ensure that you will be successful in your hiring efforts. An effective hiring process does that.

The terminology around hiring employees is jargon-based, confusing and not very helpful. Educate yourself regarding the *entire* hiring process before beginning your search. Happy recruiting! (and interviewing and hiring!)

Power Thought
The right word, rightly defined, brings clarity and confidence to what you are doing.

MOVING FORWARD!

You've now reached the end of this book—congratulations! I trust you've gained some valuable information, tips, and insights that will help you in your hiring process. You don't want to hire just anybody...you want to hire the *right* person! The right person is the one who has a passion for your company and the position being offered. This person will be full of energy, ideas, and deliverables and will have a positive effect on your company.

When I began to put these blogs together, I wanted to help hiring managers everywhere to see a paradigm shift in the way they interview potential employees. I wanted to help these over-worked individuals see past their ingrained process of hiring to look at the root of why they hire people. I wanted hiring managers to understand that the person needs to fit with the company culture, and not simply have the skills to fill the job positing. Finally, I wanted everyone involved in the hiring process to understand that connecting with a potential employee has to happen on a relationship level as well as a job skills level. I trust you feel I've accomplished my goals.

Whether you're preparing to hire your first person or you've been a hiring manager for a number of years, you don't want to settle for less than the best employee. Yes, there is an urgency to "fill the position." But if the urgency becomes "fill the need at any cost" you *will* pay a significant cost in wasted time, energy, and money, and have to start the hiring process over again. I want to help you avoid that predicament. You aren't just looking for good and competent people, you want to hire the right person—for the job position, for your company's culture, and for the long term.

Don't settle for the "best of the worst", you and your company desire the best of the best! When you are ready for my help, I'll be your recruiting partner, coaching and guiding you in the best ways to interview and hire your personnel. Until then, I trust you'll consider *Hire Power: Daily Tips & Insights to Boost Your Hiring Success* to be your go-to book.

Yours in hiring success!

Beth Smith

ACKNOWLEDGEMENTS

It takes a village to run a business, and here are my Village People in alphabetical order:

A-list Interviews Board of Advisors: Alan Wyngarden, Rick Taylor, Roger Crawford, and Steve Caldara. Your insights, observations and advice still guide me to this day.

A-list Interviews Clients: I am SO lucky to be able to do the work that I love every day. Thank you for allowing me the honor of working with you!

AuthorSource: Simon Presland and Mike Owens, you made publishing an easy and enjoyable process. Looking forward to books 3 and 4!

Barbara Peterka: My health and wellness elevated because of you.

Beth Boen: For your continued and unwavering support of my work.

Beth Steinmetz: You never let me play small. So therefore, I'm not. Thank you, my friend!

Casey-Rose Teri and Chris Alvanos: Without your guidance and hard work, my business would not have grown and, therefore, this book would not have happened. My success is due in large part to you.

Colleen Stanley: Your mentoring has been instrumental to my growth. You are a gift!

Focus PR and Marketing: Niki Lopez: I am so happy with the goals we are accomplishing together! Your friendship and coaching have been invaluable.

Jane Jenkins: I hope to be you when I grow up!

Kristin Lukela: The work that we are doing together is so inspiring! I can't wait to see where we land!

Lisa Haas: Your editing skills improved my writing so that I could write books. I wouldn't be here without the work you did.

Lisa Harris: Thanks for talking me off the ledge multiple times! Your practical advice has saved me many times!

Mandi Hogan: Your friendship has gotten me through some really dark times. You are a beautiful soul, and a very important part of my life. I am grateful.

Meryem Ersoz: Book club is the BEST! Thank you for slogging through some of the hardest books and life problems with me!

Phil Koffler: I know that I call you names, but without you, I would work out too hard and cause myself injury.

Randy Smith: I wouldn't do this job with anyone but you. Thank you for your dedication to A-list and to our daughter.

Tonya Auville: My hair is amazing because of you! HA! Thank you for our friendship over the last decade!

Triple D Girls: Laura Hein and Tina Ramey: Loopholes, unwashed hair, drive-by jello shots and long odds. I am looking for our mansion as we speak. You're welcome, my loves!

Vistage Group: Thank you for your endless support of tough love, advice and Kleenex. Thank you for your patience as I cried though many a monthly meeting!

WHY CAN'T I
HIRE
GOOD
PEOPLE?

LESSONS ON HOW TO HIRE BETTER

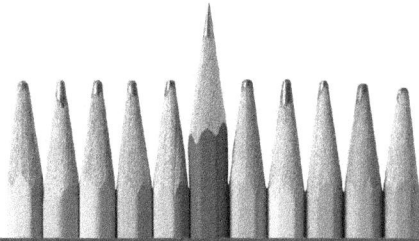

BETH SMITH

INTRODUCTION

You Have to *Learn* How to Hire Better

Your current or past hiring misfires may be less dramatic than mine, but your business is likely facing the challenge of underperforming, disruptive, or otherwise ineffective employees. According to Peter Drucker, world-renowned business consultant, two-thirds of all hiring decisions are found to be a mistake within the first year. You're certainly not alone in dealing with that issue—or with these:

- You wonder, "Why can't I hire the right people?"

- You struggle to find that perfect long-term employee who has passion for the position.

- You're uncertain about what to listen for in an interview to ensure that you have all the information you need to make a good decision.

- You get bogged down by the number of resumes you receive for an open position.

- You're unable to respond to each applicant in a timely manner.

- It seems like you should be looking for something specific in the resumes you receive.

- You wonder, "Where are all the good employees?"

- You think, "I can't hire, I don't know how to hire, and I don't know what to do about it because I still have to hire."

I provide a solution for these issues and many others you may not have bumped up against yet. My unique **Response Analysis System**™, comprises techniques that will ramp up your hiring practices—namely, the interviewing process.

The **Response Analysis System**™, simply put, is listening to the exact words of the candidate to determine if they are the right fit. This sounds easy; however, it is actually more sophisticated than you realize.

For example, imagine you have asked this question in an interview:

"Tell us about your best boss."

The candidate replies, "She was really easy to work with."

What is the most important word in that answer?

With. (You were going to say "easy," weren't you?) "With" reveals the perception the candidate had of their relationship with their boss. They did not say "easy to work *for*." An employee does not work *with* their boss; they work *for* their boss.

> ## Client Wisdom
>
> "I liked that I didn't have to say anything if I didn't want to. The process was all mapped out. Every candidate got a fair shot at succeeding or not succeeding."
>
> –Steve Caldara, President, Caldara, Wunder, and Associates

The **Response Analysis System**™ is a way to listen to a candidate's words without filters, biases, or interpretations. You have to take at face value what they say. If you don't, you end up missing the underlying communication or trying to decide if they meant something else, and that's counterproductive to the point of an interview.

You are about to learn:

- Why the current interview process doesn't work and how to fix it.

- Why we interview the way we interview.

- The psychology of the interviewer versus the interviewee.

- How to clarify your vision for a position.

- How to create an ideal candidate list.

- How to use a job description effectively.

- How to write a compelling job ad that invites the best candidates.

- How to screen and filter resumes and applications to determine interviewing fit.

- The critical components of the first, second, and third interviews.

- How to maximize a new hire's impact.

Confusion, resignation, stress, doubt, and anxiety all accompany a poor hiring decision. I know this from my own experiences and that of my clients. Such an internal state typically produces these unconstructive behaviors and attitudes:

- Hiding turnover rates because of embarrassment

- Failure to properly train new hires

- Lack of accountability

- Internal promotions without adequate clarity of expectations

- Suspicion about employee activities

And such managerial dysfunction then shows up in the workplace as lower employee morale, tense relationships between managers and staff, and reduced productivity. Ultimately, your company's viability is at risk. My objective is that you, upon turning the final page of this book, have a new or renewed confidence in your ability to make good hiring decisions that have immediate and long-term benefits for your business.

A heads-up: Please know that the **Response Analysis System™** requires a lot of work. It will not make the hiring process quicker or easier *at the beginning*—but it will be time constructively invested.

Managing a bad hire, constantly staying on top of them, putting out their fires, is the real time (and money) wasted. You necessarily spend valuable time on every new hire; I want you to do it upfront in the interview process, not on the back end micromanaging them.

It is time to revolutionize your interview process so that you find the right person the first time— every time.

Client Wisdom

"I have a new appreciation for what does and doesn't matter. I thought I was making mistakes in recruiting, but I was actually making mistakes in interviewing."

–Matt Mendez, Founder and President, SpinFusion

TESTIMONIALS

"Anyone who doesn't use this process is just plain crazy!"

~Nancy Deison, CPA
(Beth's mom)

"The next hire that I make will be the Response Analysis System™ way."

~Brad Steinmetz,
owner, Steinmetz Rental Properties

"Most places don't hire well, so they don't get the right people in place. I was hired by a great company, and I hire great people, due to the Response Analysis System™."

~Malou Van Eijk,
candidate and hiring manager

"You have to stick to this process in order for it to work. You can't just pick and choose the parts that you like."

~Dan Schachtner,
President, Concert Group Logistics

"The Response Analysis System™ forever changed how I interview."

~Lisa Harris,
23-year marketing veteran

"Thanks to the Response Analysis System™, we have such a successful operation! We are reaching goals we never dreamed were possible."

~James May,
Vice President, First Financial Bank

"I now understand the nature of the relationship between the candidate and the interviewer."

~*Jim Eddy*,
co-owner, Dream Dinners

"We have a drama- free office. People comment about how warm and relaxed it is. I wish I had done it sooner!"

~***Steve Caldara, President***, *Caldara, Wunder, and Associates*

"Morale has done a 180-degree turnaround."

~***Roger Crawford***,
President, MEP Engineering

"We have increased the quality of the people we attract, we have increased productivity, and we opened the door for growth. We have created a culture to our highest standard, all thanks to the Response Analysis System™."

~***Dr. Jon Wall, co-owner***,
Gonstead Family Chiropractic

"I now have a cohesive team. I find the right fit, and I develop them. I'm happy!"

~***Heather Castagna, Executive Director***,
Doss Heritage and Culture Center

"Before, I staffed my company with people who wanted a job. Now, I staff my company with people who are invested. I now have a profitable company."

~***Lisa Haas***,
Founder and President, Actuate Social

"I feel the current health of my business is, in a large part, due to the people you helped me find."

~***Matt Mendez***, *M.D.*,
Founder and President, SpinFusion

www.ingramcontent.com/pod-product-compliance
Lightning Source LLC
Chambersburg PA
CBHW071557210326
41597CB00019B/3283